The Haxaemeron

- ST. BASIL -

Contents:

Homily I - Page 1

Homily II - Page 23

Homily III - Page 46

Homily IV - Page 69

Homily V - Page 82

Homily VI - Page 101

Homily VII - Page 127

Homily VIII - Page 146

Homily IX - Page 169

Homily I.

In the Beginning God made the Heaven and the Earth.

1. It is right that any one beginning to narrate the formation of the world should begin with the good order which reigns in visible things. I am about to speak of the creation of heaven and earth, which was not spontaneous, as some have imagined, but drew its origin from God. What ear is worthy to hear such a tale? How earnestly the soul should prepare itself to receive such high lessons! How pure it should be from carnal affections, how unclouded by worldly disquietudes, how active and ardent in its researches, how eager to find in its surroundings an idea of God which may be worthy of Him!

But before weighing the justice of these remarks, before examining all the sense contained in these few words, let us see who addresses them to us. Because, if the weakness of our intelligence does not allow us to penetrate the depth of the thoughts of the writer, yet we shall be involuntarily drawn to give faith to his words by the force of his authority. Now it is Moses who has composed this history; Moses, who, when still at the breast, is described as exceeding fair;[1] Moses, whom the daughter of Pharaoh adopted; who received from her a royal education, and who

---

[1] Acts vii. 20, A.V.

had for his teachers the wise men of Egypt;[2] Moses, who disdained the pomp of royalty, and, to share the humble condition of his compatriots, preferred to be persecuted with the people of God rather than to enjoy the fleeting delights of sin; Moses, who received from nature such a love of justice that, even before the leadership of the people of God was committed to him, he was impelled, by a natural horror of evil, to pursue malefactors even to the point of punishing them by death; Moses, who, banished by those whose benefactor he had been, hastened to escape from the tumults of Egypt and took refuge in Ethiopia, living there far from former pursuits, and passing forty years in the contemplation of nature; Moses, finally, who, at the age of eighty, saw God, as far as it is possible for man to see Him; or rather as it had not previously been granted to man to see Him, according to the testimony of God Himself, "If there be a prophet among you, I the Lord will make myself known unto him in a vision, and will speak unto him in a dream. My servant Moses is not so, who is faithful in all mine house, with him will I speak mouth to mouth, even apparently and not in dark speeches."[3] It is this man, whom God judged worthy to behold Him, face to face, like the angels, who imparts to us what he has learnt from God. Let us listen then to these words of truth written without the help of the "enticing words of man's wisdom"[4] by the dictation of the Holy Spirit; words destined to produce not the applause of those

---

[2] cf. Joseph. ii. x. 2. So Justin M., Cohort. ad gent., Philio, Vit. Moys, and Clem. Al., Strom. i. Vide Fialon, Et. Hist. 302.

[3] Num. xii. 6, 7, 8.

[4] 1 Cor. ii. 4.

who hear them, but the salvation of those who are instructed by them.

2. "In the beginning God created the heaven and the earth."[5] I stop struck with admiration at this thought. What shall I first say? Where shall I begin my story? Shall I show forth the vanity of the Gentiles? Shall I exalt the truth of our faith? The philosophers of Greece have made much ado to explain nature, and not one of their systems has remained firm and unshaken, each being overturned by its successor. It is vain to refute them; they are sufficient in themselves to destroy one another. Those who were too ignorant to rise to a knowledge of a God, could not allow that an intelligent cause presided at the birth of the Universe; a primary error that involved them in sad consequences. Some had recourse to material principles and attributed the origin of the Universe [6] to the elements of the world. Others imagined that

---

[5] Gen. i. 1.

[6] cf. note on Letter viii. on the stoicheia or elements which the Ionian philosophers made the archai of the universe. Vide Plato, Legg. x. S: 4 and Arist., Met. i. 3.

atoms,[7] and indivisible bodies, molecules and ducts, form, by their union, the nature of the visible world. Atoms reuniting or separating, produce births and deaths and the most durable bodies only owe their consistency to the strength of their mutual adhesion: a true spider's web woven by these writers who give to heaven, to earth, and to sea so weak an origin and so little consistency! It is because they knew not how to say "In the beginning God created the heaven and the earth." Deceived by their inherent atheism it appeared to them that nothing governed or ruled the universe, and that was all was given up to chance.[8] To guard us against this error the writer on the creation, from the very first words, enlightens our understanding with the name of God; "In the beginning God created." What a glorious order! He first establishes a beginning, so that it might not be supposed that the world never had a beginning. Then he adds "Created" to show that

---

[7] Posidonius the Stoic names Moschus, or Mochus of Sidon, as the originator of the atomic theory "before the Trojan period." Vide Strabo, xvi. 757. But the most famous Atomists, Leucippus and Democritus of Abdera, in the 5th c. b.c., arose in opposition to the Eleatic school, and were followed in the 3d by Epicurus. Vide Diog. Laert. ix. S: 30, sq. and Cicero, De Nat. Deor. i. 24-26. Ista enim flagitia Democriti, sive etiam ante Leucippi, esse corpuscula quaedam laevia, alia aspera, rotunda alia, partim autem angulata, curvata quaedam, et quasi adunca; ex his effectum esse coelum atque terram, nulla cogente natura, sed concursu quodam fortuito. Atqui, si haec Democritea non audisset, quid audierat? quid est in physicis Epicuri non a Democrito? Nam, etsi quaedam commodavit, ut, quod paulo ante de inclinatione atomorum dixi: tamen pleraque dixit eadem; atomos, inane, imagines, infinitatem locorum, innumerabilitatemque mundorum eorum ortus, interitus, omnia fere, quibus naturae ratio continetur.

[8] cf. the Fortuna gubernans of Lucretius (v. 108).

which was made was a very small part of the power of the Creator. In the same way that the potter, after having made with equal pains a great number of vessels, has not exhausted either his art or his talent; thus the Maker of the Universe, whose creative power, far from being bounded by one world, could extend to the infinite, needed only the impulse of His will to bring the immensities of the visible world into being. If then the world has a beginning, and if it has been created, enquire who gave it this beginning, and who was the Creator: or rather, in the fear that human reasonings may make you wander from the truth, Moses has anticipated enquiry by engraving in our hearts, as a seal and a safeguard, the awful name of God: "In the beginning God created"–It is He, beneficent Nature, Goodness without measure, a worthy object of love for all beings endowed with reason, the beauty the most to be desired, the origin of all that exists, the source of life, intellectual light, impenetrable wisdom, it is He who "in the beginning created heaven and earth."

3. Do not then imagine, O man! that the visible world is without a beginning; and because the celestial bodies move in a circular course, and it is difficult for our senses to define the point where the circle begins, do not believe that bodies impelled by a circular movement are, from their nature, without a beginning. Without doubt the circle (I mean the plane figure described by a single line) is beyond our perception, and it is impossible for us to find out where it begins or where it ends; but we ought not on this account to believe it to be without a beginning. Although we are not sensible of it, it really begins at some point where the draughtsman has begun to draw it at a certain

radius from the centre.[9] Thus seeing that figures which move in a circle always return upon themselves, without for a single instant interrupting the regularity of their course, do not vainly imagine to yourselves that the world has neither beginning nor end. "For the fashion of this world passeth away"[10] and "Heaven and earth shall pass away."[11] The dogmas of the end, and of the renewing of the world, are announced beforehand in these short words put at the head of the inspired history. "In the beginning God made." That which was begun in time is condemned to come to an end in time. If there has been a beginning do not doubt of the end.[12] Of what use then are geometry—the calculations of arithmetic—the study of solids and far-famed astronomy, this laborious vanity, if those who pursue them imagine that this visible world is co-eternal with the Creator of all things, with God Himself; if they attribute to this limited world, which has a material body, the same glory as to the incomprehensible and invisible nature; if they cannot conceive that a whole, of which the parts are subject to corruption and change, must of necessity end by itself submitting to the fate of its parts? But they have become "vain in their imaginations and their foolish heart was darkened. Professing themselves to be wise, they became

---

[9] Fialon refers to Aristotle (De Coelo. i. 5) on the non-infinitude of the circle. The conclusion is Oti men oun to kuklo kinoumenon ouk estin ateleuteton oud' apeiron, all' echei telos, phaneron

[10] 1 Cor. vii. 31.

[11] Matt. xxiv. 35.

[12] cf. Arist. De Coelo. i. 12, 10. Delon d' hoti kai ei geneton e phtharton, ouk a& 188;dion.

fools."[13] Some have affirmed that heaven co-exists with God from all eternity;[14] others that it is God Himself without beginning or end, and the cause of the particular arrangement of all things.[15]

4. One day, doubtless, their terrible condemnation will be the greater for all this worldly wisdom, since, seeing so clearly into vain sciences, they have wilfully shut their eyes to the knowledge of the truth. These men who measure the distances of the stars and describe them, both those of the North, always shining brilliantly in our view, and those of the southern pole visible to the inhabitants of the South, but unknown to us; who divide the Northern zone and the circle of the Zodiac into an infinity of parts, who observe with exactitude the course of the stars, their fixed places, their declensions, their return and the time that each takes to make its revolution; these men, I say, have discovered all except one thing: the

---

[13] Rom. i. 21, 22.

[14] Arist., De Coelo. ii. 1. 1. calls it heis kai a& 188;dios. cf. the end of the Timaeus.

[15] cf. Cic., De nat. Deo. i. 14, "Cleanthes" (of Assos, c. 264 b.c., a disciple of Zeno) "autem tum ipsum mundum Deum dicit esse; tum totius naturae menti atque animo tribuit hoc nomen; tum ultimum, et altissimum, atque undique circumfusum, et extremum, omnia cingentem atque complexum, ardorem, qui aether nominetur, certissimum Deum judicat," and id. 15, "Chrysippus" (of Tarsus, c. 212 b.c.)..."ipsum mundum Deum dicit esse." Yet the Hymn of Cleanthes (apud Stoboeum) begins: Kudist' athanaton, poluonome, pankrates aiei, Zeus, phuseos archege, nomon meta panta kubernon. cf. Orig., v. Celsum V. saphos de ton holon kosmon (Ellenes) legousin einai theon, Stoikoi men ton proton. oi d' apo Platonos ton deuteron, tines d' auton ton triton; and Athan., De Incarn. S: 2.

fact that God is the Creator of the universe, and the just Judge who rewards all the actions of life according to their merit. They have not known how to raise themselves to the idea of the consummation of all things, the consequence of the doctrine of judgment, and to see that the world must change if souls pass from this life to a new life. In reality, as the nature of the present life presents an affinity to this world, so in the future life our souls will enjoy a lot conformable to their new condition. But they are so far from applying these truths, that they do but laugh when we announce to them the end of all things and the regeneration of the age. Since the beginning naturally precedes that which is derived from it, the writer, of necessity, when speaking to us of things which had their origin in time, puts at the head of his narrative these words—"In the beginning God created."

5. It appears, indeed, that even before this world an order of things[16] existed of which our mind can form an idea, but of which we can say nothing, because it is too lofty a subject for men who are but beginners and are still babes in knowledge. The birth of the world was preceded by a condition of things suitable for the exercise of supernatural powers, outstripping the limits of time, eternal and infinite. The Creator and Demiurge of the universe perfected His works in it, spiritual light for the happiness of all who love the Lord, intellectual and invisible natures, all the orderly arrangement[17] of pure intelligences who are beyond the reach of our mind and of whom we cannot even discover the names. They fill the essence of this

---

[16] cf. Origen, De Principiis, ii. 1, 3.

[17] diakosmesis. cf. Arist., Met. i. 5, 2.

invisible world, as Paul teaches us. "For by him were all things created that are in heaven, and that are in earth, visible and invisible whether they be thrones or dominions or principalities or powers"[18] or virtues or hosts of angels or the dignities of archangels. To this world at last it was necessary to add a new world, both a school and training place where the souls of men should be taught and a home for beings destined to be born and to die. Thus was created, of a nature analogous to that of this world and the animals and plants which live thereon, the succession of time, for ever pressing on and passing away and never stopping in its course. Is not this the nature of time, where the past is no more, the future does not exist, and the present escapes before being recognised? And such also is the nature of the creature which lives in time,–condemned to grow or to perish without rest and without certain stability. It is therefore fit that the bodies of animals and plants, obliged to follow a sort of current, and carried away by the motion which leads them to birth or to death, should live in the midst of surroundings whose nature is in accord with beings subject to change.[19] Thus the writer who wisely tells us of the birth of the Universe does not fail to put these words at the head of the narrative. "In the

---

[18] Col. i. 16.

[19] cf. Plato, Timaeus, S: 14, chronos d' oun met' ouranou gegonen hina hama gennethentes hama kai luthosin, an pote lusis tis auton gignetai kai kata to paradeigma tes aionias phuseos hin, hos homoiotatos auto kata dunamin e Fialon (p. 311) quotes Cousin's translation at greater length, and refers also to Plotinus, Enn. II. vii. 10-12. The parallel transistoriness of time and things has become the commonplace of poets. "Immortalia ne speres monet annus et almun Quae rapit hora diem." Hor.,Carm. iv. 7.

beginning God created;" that is to say, in the beginning of time. Therefore, if he makes the world appear in the beginning, it is not a proof that its birth has preceded that of all other things that were made. He only wishes to tell us that, after the invisible and intellectual world, the visible world, the world of the senses, began to exist.

The first movement is called beginning. "To do right is the beginning of the good way."[20] Just actions are truly the first steps towards a happy life. Again, we call "beginning" the essential and first part from which a thing proceeds, such as the foundation of a house, the keel of a vessel; it is in this sense that it is said, "The fear of the Lord is the beginning of wisdom,"[21] that is to say that piety is, as it were, the groundwork and foundation of perfection. Art is also the beginning of the works of artists, the skill of Bezaleel began the adornment of the tabernacle.[22] Often even the good which is the final cause is the beginning of actions. Thus the approbation of God is the beginning of almsgiving, and the end laid up for us in the promises the beginning of all virtuous efforts.

6. Such being the different senses of the word beginning, see if we have not all the meanings here.

---

[20] Prov. xvi. 5, LXX.

[21] Prov. ix. 10.

[22] cf. Arist., Met. iv. 1. Arche he men legetai hothen an ti tou pragmatos kinetheie proton; hoion tou mekous, kai hodou...he de hothen an kallista hekaston genoito; hoion kai matheseos, ouk apo tou protou kai tes tou pragmatos arches eniote arkteon, all' hothen rast' an mathoi, he de, hothen proton ginetai enuparchontos; hoion hos ploiou tropis, kai oikias themelios.

The Haxaemeron - St Basil

You may know the epoch when the formation of this world began, it, ascending into the past, you endeavour to discover the first day. You will thus find what was the first movement of time; then that the creation of the heavens and of the earth were like the foundation and the groundwork, and afterwards that an intelligent reason, as the word beginning indicates, presided in the order of visible things. [23] You will finally discover that the world was not conceived by chance and without reason, but for an useful end and for the great advantage of all beings, since it is really the school where reasonable souls exercise themselves, the training ground where they learn to know God; since by the sight of visible and sensible things the mind is led, as by a hand, to the contemplation of invisible things. "For," as the Apostle says, "the invisible things of him from the creation of the world are clearly seen, being understood by the things that are made." [24] Perhaps these words "In the beginning God created" signify the rapid and imperceptible moment of creation. The beginning, in effect, is indivisible and instantaneous. The beginning of the road is not yet the road, and that of the house is not yet the house; so the beginning of time is not yet time and not even the least particle of it. If some

---

[23] In the Homily of Origen extant in the Latin of Rufinus (Migne Pat. Gr. xii. 146) arche is used of the Divine Word, "In principio. Quod est omnium principium nisi Dominus noster Christus Iesus?...In hoc ergo principio, hoc est in Verbo suo, Deus coelum et terram fecit." An interpretation of John viii. 25, ten archen hoti kai lalo humin widely prevalent at all events in the Latin church, was "Initium quod et loquor vobis;" "I am the Beginning, that which I am even saying to you." See note to Sp. Comment. on John viii. ad fin.

[24] Rom. i. 20.

objector tell us that the beginning is a time, he ought then, as he knows well, to submit it to the division of time—a beginning, a middle and an end. Now it is ridiculous to imagine a beginning of a beginning. Further, if we divide the beginning into two, we make two instead of one, or rather make several, we really make an infinity, for all that which is divided is divisible to the infinite. [25] Thus then, if it is said, "In the beginning God created," it is to teach us that at the will of God the world arose in less than an instant, and it is to convey this meaning more clearly that other interpreters have said: "God made summarily" that is to say all at once and in a moment. [26] But enough concerning the beginning, if only to put a few points out of many.

7. Among arts, some have in view production, some practice, others theory.[27] The object of the last is the exercise of thought, that of the second, the motion of the body. Should it cease, all stops; nothing more is to be seen. Thus dancing and music have nothing behind; they have no object but themselves. In creative arts on the contrary the work lasts after the operation. Such is architecture—such are the arts which work in wood and brass and weaving, all those indeed which, even when the artisan has disappeared, serve to show an industrious intelligence and to cause the architect, the worker in

---

[25] On the inconceivability either of an absolute minimum of space or of its infinite divisibility, cf. Sir Wm. Hamilton, Met. ii. 371.

[26] Aquila's version in the Hexapla of Origen for en arche has en kephalai& 251; ektisen.

[27] he hapasa dianoia e praktike e poietike e theoretike. Arist., Met. v. i.

The Haxaemeron - St Basil

brass or the weaver, to be admired on account of his work. Thus, then, to show that the world is a work of art displayed for the beholding of all people; to make them know Him who created it, Moses does not use another word. "In the beginning," he says "God created." He does not say "God worked," "God formed," but "God created." Among those who have imagined that the world co-existed with God from all eternity, many have denied that it was created by God, but say that it exists spontaneously, as the shadow of this power. God, they say, is the cause of it, but an involuntary cause, as the body is the cause of the shadow and the flame is the cause of the brightness. [28] It is to correct this error that the prophet states, with so much precision, "In the beginning God created." He did not make the thing itself the cause of its existence.[29] Being good, He made it an useful work. Being wise, He made it everything that was

---

[28] The one and the perfect continually overflows, and from it Being, Reason, and Life are perpetually derived, without deducting anything from its substance, inasmuch as it is simple in its nature, and not, like matter, compound. (Enn. iv. ix. 9.) This derivation of all things from unity does not resemble creation, which has reference to time, but takes place purely in conformity with the principles of causality and order, without volition, because to will is to change. (Enn. iv. 5, i. 6)" Tennemann on Plotinus, Hist. Phil. S: 207.

[29] The Ben. note is "neque idipsum in causa fuit cur esset, hoc est, non res caeca, non res coacta, non res invite et praeter voluntatem agens in causa fuit cur mundus exstiterit. Hoc igitur dicit Basilius Deum aliter agere atque corpora opaca aut lucida. Nam corpus producit umbram vi atque necessitate, nec liberius agit corpus lucidum: Deus vero omnia nutu conficit et voluntate. Illud epoiesen, etc., alio modo intellexit et interpretatus est Eustathius. Illius subjicimus verba: non causam praestitit ut esset solum, sed fecit ut bonus utilem."

most beautiful. Being powerful He made it very great. [30] Moses almost shows us the finger of the supreme artisan taking possession of the substance of the universe, forming the different parts in one perfect accord, and making a harmonious symphony result from the whole.[31]

"In the beginning God made heaven and earth." By naming the two extremes, he suggests the substance of the whole world, according to heaven the privilege of seniority, and putting earth in the second rank. All intermediate beings were created at the same time as the extremities. Thus, although there is no mention of the elements, fire, water and air, [32] imagine that they were all compounded together, and you will find water, air and fire, in the earth. For fire leaps out from stones; iron which is dug from the earth produces under friction fire in plentiful measure. A marvellous fact! Fire shut up in bodies lurks there hidden without harming them, but no sooner is it released than it consumes that which has hitherto preserved it. The earth contains water, as diggers of wells teach us. It contains air too, as is shown by the vapours that it exhales under the sun's warmth [33] when it is damp.

---

[30] cf. Plat., Tim. S: 10. 'Agathos en, agatho de oudeis peri oudenos oudepote engignetai phthonos, toutou d' ektos on panta hoti malista genesthai eboulethe paraplesia heauto.

[31] cf. Huxley, Lay Sermons, xii. p. 286, on the "delicate finger" of the "hidden artist" in the changes in an egg.

[32] cf. note on Letter viii.

[33] phamen de pur kai a& 153;ra kai hudor gignesthai ex allelon kai hekaston en hekasto huparchein touton dunamei. Arist., Meteor. i. 3.

Now, as according to their nature, heaven occupies the higher and earth the lower position in space, (one sees, in fact, that all which is light ascends towards heaven, and heavy substances fall to the ground); as therefore height and depth are the points the most opposed to each other it is enough to mention the most distant parts to signify the inclusion of all which fills up intervening Space. Do not ask, then, for an enumeration of all the elements; guess, from what Holy Scripture indicates, all that is passed over in silence.

8. "In the beginning God created the heaven and the earth." If we were to wish to discover the essence of each of the beings which are offered for our contemplation, or come under our senses, we should be drawn away into long digressions, and the solution of the problem would require more words than I possess, to examine fully the matter. To spend time on such points would not prove to be to the edification of the Church. Upon the essence of the heavens we are contented with what Isaiah says, for, in simple language, he gives us sufficient idea of their nature, "The heaven was made like smoke," [34] that is to say, He created a subtle substance, without solidity or density, from which to form the heavens. As to the form of them we also content ourselves with the language of the same prophet, when praising God "that stretcheth out the heavens as a curtain and spreadeth them out as a tent to dwell in." [35] In the same way, as concerns the earth, let us resolve not to torment ourselves by trying to find out its essence, not

---

[34] Isa. li. 6, LXX.

[35] Isa. xl. 22, LXX.

The Haxaemeron - St Basil

to tire our reason by seeking for the substance which it conceals. Do not let us seek for any nature devoid of qualities by the conditions of its existence, but let us know that all the phenomena with which we see it clothed regard the conditions of its existence and complete its essence. Try to take away by reason each of the qualities it possesses, and you will arrive at nothing. Take away black, cold, weight, density, the qualities which concern taste, in one word all these which we see in it, and the substance vanishes.[36]

If I ask you to leave these vain questions, I will not expect you to try and find out the earth's point of support. The mind would reel on beholding its reasonings losing themselves without end. Do you say that the earth reposes on a bed of air?[37] How, then, can this soft substance, without consistency, resist the enormous weight which presses upon it? How is it that it does not slip away in all directions, to avoid the sinking weight, and to spread itself over the mass which overwhelms it? Do you suppose that

---

[36] Fialon points to the coincidence with Arist., Met. vii. 3. 'Alla men aphairoumenou mekous kai platous kai bathous, ouden horomen hupoleipomenon plen e& 176; ti esti to horizomenon hupo touton, hoste ten hulen ananke phainesthai monen ousian houto skopoumenois. Lego d' hulen e kath' hauten mete ti, mete poson, mete allo meden legetai hois horistai to on; esti gar ti kath' hou kategoreitai touton hekaston, ho to einai heteron, kai ton kategoreon hekaste. Ta men gar alla tes ousias kategoreitai; haute de, tes hules. & 169;Oste to eschaton, kath' hauto oute ti, oute poson, oute allo ouden estin; oude de ai apophaseis

[37] cf. Arist., De Coelo. ii. 13, 16. 'Anaximenes de kai 'Anaxagoras kai Demokritos to platos aition einai phasi tou menein auten; ou gar temnein all' epipomatizein (covers like a lid) ton a& 153;ra ton katothen, hoper phainetai ta platos echonta ton somaton poiein

The Haxaemeron - St Basil

water is the foundation of the earth? [38] You will then always have to ask yourself how it is that so heavy and opaque a body does not pass through the water; how a mass of such a weight is held up by a nature weaker than itself. Then you must seek a base for the waters, and you will be in much difficulty to say upon what the water itself rests.

9. Do you suppose that a heavier body prevents the earth from falling into the abyss? Then you must consider that this support needs itself a support to prevent it from falling. Can we imagine one? Our reason again demands yet another support, and thus we shall fall into the infinite, always imagining a base for the base which we have already found.[39] And the further we advance in this reasoning the greater force we are obliged to give to this base, so that it may be able to support all the mass weighing upon it. Put then a limit to your thought, so that your curiosity in investigating the incomprehensible may not incur the reproaches of Job, and you be not asked by him, "Whereupon are the foundations thereof fastened?"[40] If ever you hear in the Psalms, "I bear up the pillars of

---

[38] The theory of Thales. cf. note on Letter viii. 2 and Arist., De Coelo. ii. 13, 13 where he speaks of Thales describing the earth floating like wood on water.

[39] cf. Arist., De Coelo. ii. 13 (Grote's tr.): "The Kolophonian Xenophanes affirmed that the lower depths of the earth were rooted downwards to infinity, in order to escape the troublesome obligation of looking for a reason why it remained stationary." To this Empedokles objected, and suggested velocity of rotation for the cause of the earth's maintaining its position.

[40] Job xxxviii. 6.

The Haxaemeron - St Basil

it;"⁴¹ see in these pillars the power which sustains it. Because what means this other passage, "He hath founded it upon the sea," ⁴² if not that the water is spread all around the earth? How then can water, the fluid element which flows down every declivity, remain suspended without ever flowing? You do not reflect that the idea of the earth suspended by itself throws your reason into a like but even greater difficulty, since from its nature it is heavier. But let us admit that the earth rests upon itself, or let us say that it rides the waters, we must still remain faithful to thought of true religion and recognise that all is sustained by the Creator's power. Let us then reply to ourselves, and let us reply to those who ask us upon what support this enormous mass rests, "In His hands are the ends of the earth."⁴³ It is a doctrine as infallible for our own information as profitable for our hearers.

10. There are inquirers into nature⁴⁴ who with a great display of words give reasons for the immobility of the earth. Placed, they say, in the middle of the universe and not being able to incline more to one side than the other because its centre is everywhere the same distance from the surface, it necessarily rests upon itself; since a weight which is everywhere equal cannot lean to either side. It is not, they go on, without reason or by chance that the earth occupies the

---

[41] Ps. lxxv. 3.

[42] Ps. xxiv. 2.

[43] Ps. xcv. 4, LXX.

[44] hoi phusikoi was the name given to the Ionic and other philosophers who preceded Socrates. Lucian (Ner. 4) calls Thales phusikotatos.

The Haxaemeron - St Basil

centre of the universe. It is its natural and necessary position. As the celestial body occupies the higher extremity of space all heavy bodies, they argue, that we may suppose to have fallen from these high regions, will be carried from all directions to the centre, and the point towards which the parts are tending will evidently be the one to which the whole mass will be thrust together. If stones, wood, all terrestrial bodies, fall from above downwards, this must be the proper and natural place of the whole earth. If, on the contrary, a light body is separated from the centre, it is evident that it will ascend towards the higher regions. Thus heavy bodies move from the top to the bottom, and following this reasoning, the bottom is none other than the centre of the world. Do not then be surprised that the world never falls: it occupies the centre of the universe, its natural place. By necessity it is obliged to remain in its place, unless a movement contrary to nature should displace it.[45] If there is anything in this system which might appear probable to you, keep your admiration for the source of such perfect order, for the wisdom of God. Grand phenomena do not strike us the less when we have discovered something of their wonderful mechanism. Is it otherwise here? At all events let us prefer the simplicity of faith to the demonstrations of reason.

11. We might say the same thing of the heavens. With what a noise of words the sages of this world have discussed their nature! Some have said that heaven is composed of four elements as being tangible and visible, and is made up of earth on account of its

---

[45] cf. De Coelo. ii. 14, 4. Eti d' he phora ton morion kai holes autes e kata phusin epi to meson tou pantos estin, dia touto gar kai tunchanei keimene nun epi tou kentrou.

power of resistance, with fire because it is striking to the eye, with air and water on account of the mixture.[46] Others have rejected this system as improbable, and introduced into the world, to form the heavens, a fifth element after their own fashioning. There exists, they say, an aethereal body which is neither fire, air, earth, nor water, nor in one word any simple body. These simple bodies have their own natural motion in a straight line, light bodies upwards and heavy bodies downwards; now this motion upwards and downwards is not the same as circular motion; there is the greatest possible difference between straight and circular motion. It therefore follows that bodies whose motion is so various must vary also in their essence. But, it is not even possible to suppose that the heavens should be formed of primitive bodies which we call elements, because the reunion of contrary forces could not produce an even and spontaneous motion, when each of the simple bodies is receiving a different impulse from nature. Thus it is a labour to maintain composite bodies in continual movement, because it is impossible to put even a single one of their movements in accord and harmony with all those that are in discord; since what is proper to the light particle, is in warfare with that of a heavier one. If we attempt to rise we are stopped by the weight of the terrestrial element; if we throw ourselves down we violate the igneous part of our being in dragging it down contrary to its nature. Now this struggle of the elements effects their dissolution. A body to which violence is done and which is placed in opposition to nature, after a short but energetic resistance, is soon dissolved into as many parts as it

---

[46] This is the doctrine of Plato vide Tim. The Combef. mss. reads not mixis, mixture, but methexis, participation.

The Haxaemeron - St Basil

had elements, each of the constituent parts returning to its natural place. It is the force of these reasons, say the inventors of the fifth kind of body for the genesis of heaven and the stars, which constrained them to reject the system of their predecessors and to have recourse to their own hypothesis.[47] But yet another fine speaker arises and disperses and destroys this theory to give predominance to an idea of his own invention.

Do not let us undertake to follow them for fear of falling into like frivolities; let them refute each other, and, without disquieting ourselves about essence, let us say with Moses "God created the heavens and the earth." Let us glorify the supreme Artificer for all that

---

[47] Here appears to be a reference to Arist., De Gen. Ann. ii. 3, 11, pases men oun psuches dunamis heteron somatos e& 231;ike kekoinonekenai kai theioterou ton kaloumenon stoicheion; hos de diapherousi timioteti hai psuchai kai atimi& 139; allelon houto kai he toiaute diapherei phusis, and again, pneuma...analogon ousa to ton astron stoichei& 251;. On the fifth element of Aristotle cf. Cic., Tusc. Disp. i. 10. Aristoteles...cum quatuor illa genera principiorum erat complexus, equibus omnia orirentur, quintam quandam naturam censet esse, equa sit mens. Aug., De Civ. Dei xxii. 11. 2, and Cudworth's Int. Syst. (Harrison's Ed. 1845) iii. p. 465. Hence the word "quintessence," for which the Dictionaries quote Howard's Translation of Plutarch, "Aristoteles hath put...for elements foure; and for a fifth quintessence, the heavenly body which is immutable." Skeat s. v. points out that "the idea is older than Aristotle: cf. the five Skt. bhutas, or elements, which were earth, air, fire, and water, and aether. Thus the fifth essence is aether, the subtlest and highest." It is evident that Milton had these theories in mind when he wrote (Par. Lost, iii. 716): "Swift to their several quarters hasted then The cumbrous elements, earth, flood, air, fire; And this ethereal quintessence of heaven Flew upward, spirited with various forms, That rolled orbicular, and turned to stars Numberless."

was wisely and skillfully made; by the beauty of visible things let us raise ourselves to Him who is above all beauty; by the grandeur of bodies, sensible and limited in their nature, let us conceive of the infinite Being whose immensity and omnipotence surpass all the efforts of the imagination. Because, although we ignore the nature of created things, the objects which on all sides attract our notice are so marvellous, that the most penetrating mind cannot attain to the knowledge of the least of the phenomena of the world, either to give a suitable explanation of it or to render due praise to the Creator, to Whom belong all glory, all honour and all power world without end. Amen.

Homily II

"The Earth was Invisible and Unfinished." [48]

1. In the few words which have occupied us this morning we have found such a depth of thought that we despair of penetrating further. If such is the fore court of the sanctuary, if the portico of the temple is so grand and magnificent, if the splendour of its beauty thus dazzles the eyes of the soul, what will be the holy of holies? Who will dare to try to gain access to the innermost shrine? Who will look into its secrets? To gaze into it is indeed forbidden us, and language is powerless to express what the mind conceives. However, since there are rewards, and most desirable ones, reserved by the just Judge for the intention alone of doing good, do not let us hesitate to continue our researches. Although we may not attain to the truth, if, with the help of the Spirit, we do not fall away from the meaning of Holy Scripture we shall not deserve to be rejected, and, with the help of grace, we shall contribute to the edification of the Church of God.

"The earth," says Holy Scripture, "was invisible and unfinished." The heavens and the earth were created without distinction. How then is it that the heavens are perfect whilst the earth is still unformed and incomplete? In one word, what was the unfinished condition of the earth? And for what reason was it invisible? The fertility of the earth is its perfect finishing; growth of all kinds of plants, the upspringing

---

[48] Gen. i. 2, LXX.

of tall trees, both productive and sterile, flowers' sweet scents and fair colours, and all that which, a little later, at the voice of God came forth from the earth to beautify her, their universal Mother. As nothing of all this yet existed, Scripture is right in calling the earth "without form." We could also say of the heavens that they were still imperfect and had not received their natural adornment, since at that time they did not shine with the glory of the sun and of the moon and were not crowned by the choirs of the stars.[49] These bodies were not yet created. Thus you will not diverge from the truth in saying that the heavens also were "without form." The earth was invisible for two reasons: it may be because man, the spectator, did not yet exist, or because being submerged under the waters which over-flowed the surface, it could not be seen, since the waters had not yet been gathered together into their own places, where God afterwards collected them, and gave them the name of seas. What is invisible? First of all that which our fleshly eye cannot perceive; our mind, for example; then that which, visible in its nature, is hidden by some body which conceals it, like iron in the depths of the earth. It is in this sense, because it was hidden under the waters, that the earth was still invisible. However, as light did not yet exist, and as the earth lay in darkness, because of the obscurity of the air above it, it should not astonish us that for this reason Scripture calls it "invisible."

2. But the corrupters of the truth, who, incapable of submitting their reason to Holy Scripture, distort at will

---

[49] cf. Hom., Il. xviii. 485, en de ta teirea panta ta t' ouranos estephanotai, and Tennyson's "When young night divine crowned dying day with stars." (Palace of Art.)

The Haxaemeron - St Basil

the meaning of the Holy Scriptures, pretend that these words mean matter. For it is matter, they say, which from its nature is without form and invisible,—being by the conditions of its existence without quality and without form and figure.[50] The Artificer submitting it to the working of His wisdom clothed it with a form, organized it, and thus gave being to the visible world.

If matter is uncreated, it has a claim to the same honours as God, since it must be of equal rank with Him. Is this not the summit of wickedness, that an extreme deformity, without quality, without form, shape, ugliness without configuration, to use their own expression, should enjoy the same prerogatives with Him, Who is wisdom, power and beauty itself, the Creator and the Demiurge of the universe? This is not all. If matter is so great as to be capable of being acted on by the whole wisdom of God, it would in a way raise its hypostasis to an equality with the inaccessible power of God, since it would be able to measure by itself all the extent of the divine intelligence. If it is insufficient for the operations of

---

[50] On prime matter and its being asomatos and amorphos vide Cudworth, Int. Syst. v. ii. S: 27, and Mosheim's note. "Ingens vero quondam summorum et inclytorum virorum numerus ab eorum semper stetit partibus, quibus ex qua dixi ratione, materiam placuit decernere asomaton esse, si'e chorpore charere Chichero omnes post Platonem peilosopeos eoch dogma pereibet tenuisse, Achad. Thust. i. 7, sed subechtam putant omnibus sine ulla spechie, atthue charentem omni illa thualitate materiam thuandam ex thua omnia expressa atthue ephphechta sint.' Sed am diu ante Platonem Ppsteagororum multi ei addichti phuerunt, thuod exTimaei Locri, nobilis hujus scholae et perantiqui philosophi, De Anima Mundi libello (Cap. i. p. 544, Ed. Galei) intelligitur: tan hulan amorphon de kath' autan kai achrematiston dechomenon de pasan morphan."

God, then we fall into a more absurd blasphemy, since we condemn God for not being able, on account of the want of matter, to finish His own works. The poverty of human nature has deceived these reasoners. Each of our crafts is exercised upon some special matter–the art of the smith upon iron, that of the carpenter on wood. In all, there is the subject, the form and the work which results from the form. Matter is taken from without–art gives the form–and the work is composed at the same time of form and of matter.[51]

Such is the idea that they make for themselves of the divine work. The form of the world is due to the wisdom of the supreme Artificer; matter came to the Creator from without; and thus the world results from a double origin. It has received from outside its matter and its essence, and from God its form and figure.[52] They thus come to deny that the mighty God has presided at the formation of the universe, and pretend that He has only brought a crowning contribution to a common work, that He has only contributed some small portion to the genesis of beings: they are incapable from the debasement of their reasonings of raising their glances to the height of truth. Here below arts are subsequent to matter–introduced into life by the indispensable need of them. Wool existed before weaving made it supply one of nature's imperfections. Wood existed before carpentering took possession of

---

[51] cf. Arist., Met. vi. 7, panta de ta gignomena hupo te tinos gignetai, kai ek tinos, kai ti...to de ex hou gignetai, hen legomen hulen...to de huph' hou, ton phusei ti onton...eidos de lego to ti en einai hekaston, kai ten proten ousian.

[52] cf. Cudworth, Int. Syst. iv. 6, and remarks there on Cic., Acad Quaest. i. 6. Arist. (Metaph. i. 2) says Theos gar dokei to aition pasin einai kai arche tis, but does this refer only to form?

it, and transformed it each day to supply new wants, and made us see all the advantages derived from it, giving the oar to the sailor, the winnowing fan to the labourer, the lance to the soldier. But God, before all those things which now attract our notice existed, after casting about in His mind and determining to bring into being time which had no being, imagined the world such as it ought to be, and created matter in harmony with the form which He wished to give it.[53] He assigned to the heavens the nature adapted for the heavens, and gave to the earth an essence in accordance with its form. He formed, as He wished, fire, air and water, and gave to each the essence which the object of its existence required. Finally, He welded all the diverse parts of the universe by links of indissoluble attachment and established between them so perfect a fellowship and harmony that the most distant, in spite of their distance, appeared united in one universal sympathy. Let those men therefore renounce their fabulous imaginations, who, in spite of the weakness of their argument, pretend to measure a power as incomprehensible to man's reason as it is unutterable by man's voice.

3. God created the heavens and the earth, but not only half;—He created all the heavens and all the earth, creating the essence with the form. For He is not an inventor of figures, but the Creator even of the essence of beings. Further let them tell us how the efficient power of God could deal with the passive nature of matter, the latter furnishing the matter without form, the former possessing the science of the

---

[53] Gen. ii. 5, "every herb of the field before it grew." There seems here an indication of the actual creation, poiesis, being in the mind of God.

form without matter, both being in need of each other; the Creator in order to display His art, matter in order to cease to be without form and to receive a form.[54] But let us stop here and return to our subject.

"The earth was invisible and unfinished." In saying "In the beginning God created the heavens and the earth," the sacred writer passed over many things in silence, water, air, fire and the results from them,

---

[54] Fialon quotes Bossuet: "Je ne trouve point que Dieu, qui a cree toutes choses, ait eu besoin, comme un ouvrier vulgaire, de trouver une matiere preparee sur laquelle il travaillat, et de laquelle il dit son ouvrage. Mais, n'ayant besoin pour agir que de lui-meme et de sa propre puissance il a fait tout son ouvrage. Il n'est point un simple faiseur de formes et de figures dans une matiere preexistante; il a fait et la matiere et la forme, c'est-`a-dire son ouvrage dans son tout: autrement son ouvrage ne lui doit pas tout, et dans son fond il est independamment de son ouvrier.... "O Dieu quelle a ete l'ignorance des sages du monde, qu'on a appeles philosophes d'avoir cru que vous, parfait architecte et absolu formateur de tout ce qui est, vous aviez trouve sous vos mains une matiere qui vous otait co-eternelle, informe neamoins, et qui attendait de vous sa perfection! Aveugles, qui n'entendaient pas que d'etre capable de forme, c'est deja quelque forme; c'est quelque perfection, que d'etre capable de perfection; et si la matiere avail d'elle-meme ce commencement de perfection et de forme, elle en pouvait aussitot avoir d'ellememe l'entier accomplissement. "Aveugles, conducteurs d'aveugles, qui tombez dans le precipice, et y jetez ceux qui vous suivent (St. Matthieu xv. 14), dites-moi qui a assujeti `a Dieu ce qu'il n'a pas fait, ce qui est de soi aussi bien que Dieu, ce qui est independamment de Dieu meme? Par ou a-t-il trouve prise sur ce qui lui est etranger et independant et sa puissance; et par quel art ou quel pouvoir se l'est-il soumis?... Mais qu'est-ce apres tout que cette matiere si parfait, qu'elle ait elle-meme ce fond de son etre; et si imparfaite, qu'elle attende sa perfection d'un autre? Dieu aura fait l'accident et n'aura pas fait la substance? (Bossuet, Elevations sur les mysteres, 3e semaine, 2e elevat.)

The Haxaemeron - St Basil

which, all forming in reality the true complement of the world, were, without doubt, made at the same time as the universe. By this silence, history wishes to train the activity or our intelligence, giving it a weak point for starting, to impel it to the discovery of the truth. Thus, we are not told of the creation of water; but, as we are told that the earth was invisible, ask yourself what could have covered it, and prevented it from being seen? Fire could not conceal it. Fire brightens all about it, and spreads light rather than darkness around. No more was it air that enveloped the earth. Air by nature is of little density and transparent. It receives all kinds of visible object, and transmits them to the spectators. Only one supposition remains; that which floated on the surface of the earth was water– the fluid essence which had not yet been confined to its own place. Thus the earth was not only invisible; it was still incomplete. Even today excessive damp is a hindrance to the productiveness of the earth. The same cause at the same time prevents it from being seen, and from being complete, for the proper and natural adornment of the earth is its completion: corn waving in the valleys–meadows green with grass and rich with many coloured flowers–fertile glades and hill-tops shaded by forests. Of all this nothing was yet produced; the earth was in travail with it in virtue of the power that she had received from the Creator. But she was waiting for the appointed time and the divine order to bring forth.

4. "Darkness was upon the face of the deep."[55] A new source for fables and most impious imaginations if one distorts the sense of these words at the will of

---

[55] Gen. i. 2.

The Haxaemeron - St Basil

one's fancies. By "darkness" these wicked men do not understand what is meant in reality–air not illumined, the shadow produced by the interposition of a body, or finally a place for some reason deprived of light. For them "darkness" is an evil power, or rather the personification of evil, having his origin in himself in opposition to, and in perpetual struggle with, the goodness of God. If God is light, they say, without any doubt the power which struggles against Him must be darkness, "Darkness" not owing its existence to a foreign origin, but an evil existing by itself. "Darkness" is the enemy of souls, the primary cause of death, the adversary of virtue. The words of the Prophet, they say in their error, show that it exists and that it does not proceed from God. From this what perverse and impious dogmas have been imagined! What grievous wolves,[56] tearing the flock of the Lord, have sprung from these words to cast themselves upon souls! Is it not from hence that have come forth Marcions and Valentini,[57] and the detestable heresy of the

---

[56] Acts xx. 29.

[57] Marcion and Valentinus are roughly lumped together as types of gnostic dualism. On the distinction between their systems see Dr. Salmon in D.C.B. iii. 820. Marcion, said to have been the son of a bishop of Sinope, is the most Christian of the gnostics, and "tries to fit in his dualism with the Christian creed and with the scriptures." But he expressly "asserted the existence of two Gods." The Valentinian ideas and emanations travelled farther afield.

The Haxaemeron - St Basil

Manicheans,[58] which you may without going far wrong call the putrid humour of the churches.

O man, why wander thus from the truth, and imagine for thyself that which will cause thy perdition? The word is simple and within the comprehension of all. "The earth was invisible." Why? Because the "deep" was spread over its surface. What is "the deep"? A mass of water of extreme depth. But we know that we can see many bodies through clear and transparent water. How then was it that no part of the earth appeared through the water? Because the air which surrounded it was still without light and in darkness. The rays of the sun, penetrating the water, often allow us to see the pebbles which form the bed of the river, but in a dark night it is impossible for our glance to penetrate under the water. Thus, these words "the earth was invisible" are explained by those that follow; "the deep" covered it and itself was in darkness. Thus, the deep is not a multitude of hostile powers, as has been imagined;[59] nor "darkness" an evil sovereign force in enmity with good. In reality two rival principles of equal power, if engaged without ceasing in a war of mutual attacks, will end in self destruction. But if one

---

[58] On Manicheism, videBeausobre's Critical History of Manicheism, and Walch, Hist. Ketz. i. 770. With its theory of two principles it spread widely over the empire in the 4th c., was vigorous in Armenia in the 9th, and is said to have appeared in France in the 12th. (cf. Bayle, Dict. s.v.) On the view taken of the heresy in Basil's time cf. Gregory of Nyssa, Against Eunomius i. S: 35.

[59] i.e. by those who would identify the abussos (Tehom) of Gen. i. 2 with that of Luke i. 31, and understand it to mean the abode in prison of evil spirits. The Hebrew word occurs in Job xxviii. 14 and Deut. xxxiii. 13 for the depth of waters.

should gain the mastery it would completely annihilate the conquered. Thus, to maintain the balance in the struggle between good and evil is to represent them as engaged in a war without end and in perpetual destruction, where the opponents are at the same time conquerors and conquered. If good is the stronger, what is there to prevent evil being completely annihilated? But if that be the case, the very utterance of which is impious, I ask myself how it is that they themselves are not filled with horror to think that they have imagined such abominable blasphemies.

It is equally impious to say that evil has its origin from God;[60] because the contrary cannot proceed from its contrary. Life does not engender death; darkness is not the origin of light; sickness is not the maker of

---

[60] With this view Plutarch charges the Stoics. Autoi ton kakon archen agathon onta ton Theon poiousi. (c. Stoicos, 1976.) But it is his deduction from their statements—not their own statements. cf. Mosheim's note on Cudworth iv. S: 13. Origen (c. Celsum vi.) distinguishes between ten kakian kai tas ap' autes praxeis, and kakon as punitive and remedial; if the latter can rightly be called evil in any sense, God is the author of it. cf. Amos iii. 6. Vide, also, Basil's treatment of this question in his Treatise hoti ouk estin aitios ton kakon ho theos. cf. Schroeck. Kirchengeschichte xiii. 194.

health.[61] In the changes of conditions there are transitions from one condition to the contrary; but in genesis each being proceeds from its like, and not from its contrary. If then evil is neither uncreate nor created by God, from whence comes its nature? Certainly that evil exists, no one living in the world will deny. What shall we say then? Evil is not a living animated essence; it is the condition of the soul opposed to virtue, developed in the careless on account of their falling away from good.[62]

5. Do not then go beyond yourself to seek for evil, and imagine that there is an original nature of wickedness. Each of us, let us acknowledge it, is the first author of

---

[61] Fialon points out the correspondence with Plat. Phaed. S: 119, kai tis eipe ton paronton akousas...pros Then, ouk en tois prosthen hemin logois auto to enantion ton nuni legomenon homologeito, ek tou elattonos to meizon gignesthai, kai ek tou meizonos to elatton, kai atechnos haute einai he genesis tois enantiois ek ton enantion ; nun de moi dokei legesthai hoti touto ouk an pote genoito. Kai ho Sokrates ...ephe...ouk ennoeis to diapheron tou ti nun legomenou kai tou tote; tote; men gar elegeto ek tou enantiou pragmatos to enantion pragma gignesthai, nun de hoti auto to enantion heauto enantion ouk an pote genoito, oute to en hemin oute to en phusei; tote men gar peri ton echonton ton enantion elegomen, eponomazontes auta te ekeinon eponumi& 139;, nun de peri ekeinon auton hon enonton, echei ten eponumian ta onomazomena, auta d' ekeina ouk an pote phamen ethegesai genesin allelon dexasthai.

[62] "Cette phrase est prise textuellement dans Denys l'Areopagite, ou du moins dans l'ouvrage qui lui est attribue. (De Div. Nom. iv. 18. Laur. Lyd. de mensib. ed. Roeth. 186, 28.)." Fialon. In the Treatise referred to, peri Theion 'Onomaton, "evil" is said to be "nothing real and positive, but a defect, a negation only. Steresis ara esti to kakon, kai elleipsis, kai astheneia, kai asummetria." D.C.B. i. 846. cf. "Evil is null, is nought, is silence implying sound." Browning. Abt. Vogler.

his own vice. Among the ordinary events of life, some come naturally, like old age and sickness, others by chance like unforeseen occurrences, of which the origin is beyond ourselves, often sad, sometimes fortunate, as for instance the discovery of a treasure when digging a well, or the meeting of a mad dog when going to the market place. Others depend upon ourselves, such as ruling one's passions, or not putting a bridle on one's pleasures, to be master of our anger, or to raise the hand against him who irritates us, to tell the truth, or to lie, to have a sweet and well-regulated disposition, or to be fierce and swollen and exalted with pride.[63] Here you are the master of your actions. Do not look for the guiding cause beyond yourself, but recognise that evil, rightly so called, has no other origin than our voluntary falls. If it were involuntary, and did not depend upon ourselves, the laws would not have so much terror for the guilty, and the tribunals would not be so without pity when they condemn wretches according to the measure of their crimes. But enough concerning evil rightly so called. Sickness, poverty, obscurity, death, finally all human afflictions, ought not to be ranked as evils; since we do not count among the greatest

---

[63] cf. Epictetus, Ench. i. eph' hemin men hupolepsis, horme, orexis, ekklisis, kai heni logo hosa hemetera erga.

The Haxaemeron - St Basil

boons things which are their opposites. [64] Among these afflictions, some are the effect of nature, others have obviously been for many a source of advantage. Let us then be silent for the moment about these metaphors and allegories, and, simply following without vain curiosity the words of Holy Scripture, let us take from darkness the idea which it gives us.

But reason asks, was darkness created with the world? Is it older than light? Why in spite of its inferiority has it preceded it? Darkness, we reply, did not exist in essence; it is a condition produced in the air by the withdrawal of light. What then is that light which disappeared suddenly from the world, so that darkness should cover the face of the deep? If anything had existed before the formation of this sensible and perishable world, no doubt we conclude it would have been in light. The orders of angels, the heavenly hosts, all intellectual natures named or unnamed, all the ministering spirits, [65] did not live in

---

[64] cf. M. Aurelius II. xi. ho gar cheiro me poiei anthropon, pos de touto bion anthropou cheiro poieseien;...thanatos de ge kai zoe doxa kai adoxia, ponos kai hedone, ploutos kai penia, panta tauta epises sumbainei anthropon tois te agathois kai tois kakois, oute kala onta oute aischra; out' ar' agatha oute kaka esti. Also Greg. Nyss. Orat. Cat. and Aug., De Civ. Dei. i. 8. Ista vero temporalia bona et mala utrisque voluit esse communia, ut nec bona cupidius appetantur, quae mali quoque habere cernuntur, nec mala turpiter evitentur, quibus et boni plerumque afficiuntur.

[65] cf. Heb. i. 14.

darkness, but enjoyed a condition fitted for them in light and spiritual joy.[66]

No one will contradict this; least of all he who looks for celestial light as one of the rewards promised to virtue, the light which, as Solomon says, is always a light to the righteous,[67] the light which made the Apostle say "Giving thanks unto the Father, which hath made us meet to be partakers of the inheritance of the saints in light."[68] Finally, if the condemned are sent into outer darkness[69] evidently those who are made worthy of God's approval, are at rest in heavenly light. When then, according to the order of God, the heaven appeared, enveloping all that its circumference included, a vast and unbroken body separating outer things from those which it enclosed, it necessarily kept the space inside in darkness for want of communication with the outer light. Three things are, indeed, needed to form a shadow, light, a body, a dark place. The shadow of heaven forms the darkness of the world. Understand, I pray you, what I mean, by a simple example; by raising for yourself at

---

[66] cf. Theod. (Quaest. in Gen. vi.) who is ready to accept the creation of angels before the creation of the world. Origen, Hom. i. in Gen. Hom. iv. in Is. taught the existence of angels "before the aeons." Greg. Naz., Orat. xxxviii. The lxx. Trans. of Job xxxviii. 7, enesan me pantes angeloi mou may have aided in the formation of the general opinion of the Greek Fathers. The systematization of the hierarchies is due to the pseudo, Dionysius, and was transmitted to the west through John Erigena. cf. Milman, Lat. Christ. ix. 59.

[67] Prov. xiii. 9, lxx.

[68] Col. i. 12.

[69] cf. Matt. xxii. 13.

The Haxaemeron - St Basil

mid-day a tent of some compact and impenetrable material, and shutting yourself up in it in sudden darkness. Suppose that original darkness was like this, not subsisting directly by itself, but resulting from some external causes. If it is said that it rested upon the deep, it is because the extremity of air naturally touches the surface of bodies; and as at that time the water covered everything, we are obliged to say that darkness was upon the face of the deep.

6. And the Spirit of God was borne upon the face of the waters.[70] Does this spirit mean the diffusion of air? The sacred writer wishes to enumerate to you the elements of the world, to tell you that God created the heavens, the earth, water, and air and that the last was now diffused and in motion; or rather, that which is truer and confirmed by the authority of the ancients, by the Spirit of God, he means the Holy Spirit. It is, as has been remarked, the special name, the name above all others that Scripture delights to give to the Holy Spirit, and always by the spirit of God the Holy Spirit is meant, the Spirit which completes the divine and blessed Trinity. You will find it better therefore to take it in this sense. How then did the Spirit of God move upon the waters? The explanation that I am about to give you is not an original one, but that of a Syrian,[71] who was as ignorant in the wisdom of this world as he was versed in the knowledge of the Truth. He said, then, that the Syriac word was more expressive, and that being more analogous to the

---

[70] Gen. i. 2, lxxx.

[71] Tillemont understands Eusebius of Samosata. The Ben. note prefers Ephrem Syrus, and compares Jerome, Quaest. Heb. Col. 508.

Hebrew term it was a nearer approach to the scriptural sense. This is the meaning of the word; by "was borne" the Syrians, he says, understand: it cherished[72] the nature of the waters as one sees a bird cover the eggs with her body and impart to them vital force from her own warmth. Such is, as nearly as possible, the meaning of these words–the Spirit was borne: let us understand, that is, prepared the nature of water to produce living beings:[73] a sufficient proof for those who ask if the Holy Spirit took an active part in the creation of the world.

7. And God said, Let there be light.[74] The first word of God created the nature of light; it made darkness vanish, dispelled gloom, illuminated the world, and gave to all beings at the same time a sweet and gracious aspect. The heavens, until then enveloped in darkness, appeared with that beauty which they still present to our eyes. The air was lighted up, or rather

---

[72] Gen. i. 2. Vide R.V. margin. The word rachaph, "brood," is not used of wind, and itself appears to fix the meaning of the Spirit in the place. An old interpretation of the Orphic Poem Argonautica would identify the brooding Spirit of Genesis with the All Wise Love of the Greek poet: prota men archaiou chaeos megalephaton humnon, hos epameipse phuseis, hos t' ouranos es peras elthen, ges t' eurusternou genesin, puthmenas te thalasses , presbutaton te kai autotele pol metin Erota, hossa t' ephusen hapanta, ta d' e?oithen allou ap' allo. Orph., Argon. 423-427. On the translation of rachaph by "brooding," cf. Milton, P. Lost, vii.: "darkness profound Covered the abyss; but on the watery calm His brooding wings the Spirit of God outspread, And vital virtue infused, and vital warmth, Throughout the fluid mass."

[73] zoogonia. cf. De Sp. S.S: 56, and Bp. Pearson, on the Creed, Art. V.

[74] Gen. i. 3.

The Haxaemeron - St Basil

made the light circulate mixed with its substance, and, distributing its splendour rapidly in every direction, so dispersed itself to its extreme limits. Up it sprang to the very aether and heaven. In an instant it lighted up the whole extent of the world, the North and the South, the East and the West. For the aether also is such a subtle substance and so transparent that it needs not the space of a moment for light to pass through it. Just as it carries our sight instantaneously to the object of vision,[75] so without the least interval, with a rapidity that thought cannot conceive, it receives these rays of light in its uttermost limits. With light the aether becomes more pleasing and the waters more limpid. These last, not content with receiving its splendour, return it by the reflection of light and in all directions send forth quivering flashes. The divine word gives every object a more cheerful and a more attractive appearance, just as when men in deep sea pour in oil they make the place about them clear. So, with a single word and in one instant, the Creator of all things gave the boon of light to the world.[76]

---

[75] Light is said to travel straight at the rate of about 195,000 English miles a second; a velocity estimated by observations on the eclipses of Jupiter's satellites. The modern undulatory theory of light, of which Huyghens (1695) is generally regarded as the author, describes light as propagated by the vibrations of the imponderable matter termed Ether or AEther.

[76] The simile seems hardly worthy of the topic. The practice is referred to by Plutarch, Symp. Quaest. i. 9, and by Pliny, Hist. Nat. ii. 106. "Omne oleo tranquillari; et ob id urinantes ore spargere, quoniam mitiget naturam asperam lucemque deportet." "gerere" says the Delph. note, "tum credas oleum vicem conspiciliorum.

The Haxaemeron - St Basil

Let there be light. The order was itself an operation, and a state of things was brought into being, than which man's mind cannot even imagine a pleasanter one for our enjoyment. It must be well understood that when we speak of the voice, of the word, of the command of God, this divine language does not mean to us a sound which escapes from the organs of speech, a collision of air [77] struck by the tongue; it is a simple sign of the will of God, and, if we give it the form of an order, it is only the better to impress the souls whom we instruct.[78]

And God saw the light, that it was good.[79] How can we worthily praise light after the testimony given by the Creator to its goodness? The word, even among

---

[77] A statement not unlike the "Vibrations of the elastic medium," to which sound might now be referred. "Sed vocem Stoici corpus esse contendunt: eamque esse dicunt ictum aera: Plato autem non esse vocem corpus esse putat. Non enim percussus, inquit, aer, sed plaga ipsa atque percussio, vox est: ouk haplos plege aeros estin he phone; plettei gar ton aera kai daktulos paragomenos, kai oudepo poiei phonen; all' he pose plege, kai sphodra, kai tose de hoste akousten genesthai." Aul. Gell., N.A. v. 15. So Diog. Laert. in Vita Zenonis; esti phone aer peplegmenos.

[78] Fialon quotes Bossuet 4me elev. 3me sem.: "Le roi dit Qu'on marche; et l'armee marche; qu'on fasse telle evolution, et elle se fait; toute une armee se remue au seul commandement d'un prince, c'est `a dire, `a un seul petit mouvment de ces livres, c'est, parmi les choses humaines, l'image la plus excellente de la puissance de Dieu; mais au fond que c'est image est defectueuse! Dieu n'a point de levres `a remuer; Dieu ne frappe point l'air pour en tirer quelque son; Dieu n'a qu'`a vouloir en lui meme; et tout ce qu'il veut eternellement s'accomplit comme il l'a voulu, et au temps qu'il a marque.

[79] Gen. i. 4.

us, refers the judgment to the eyes, incapable of raising itself to the idea that the senses have already received.[80] But, if beauty in bodies results from symmetry of parts, and the harmonious appearance of colours, how in a simple and homogeneous essence like light, can this idea of beauty be preserved? Would not the symmetry in light be less shown in its parts than in the pleasure and delight at the sight of it? Such is also the beauty of gold, which it owes not to the happy mingling of its parts, but only to its beautiful colour which has a charm attractive to the eyes.

Thus again, the evening star is the most beautiful of the stars:[81] not that the parts of which it is composed form a harmonious whole; but thanks to the unalloyed and beautiful brightness which meets our eyes. And further, when God proclaimed the goodness of light, it was not in regard to the charm of the eye but as a provision for future advantage, because at that time there were as yet no eyes to judge of its beauty. "And God divided the light from the darkness;"[82] that is to say, God gave them natures incapable of mixing, perpetually in opposition to each other, and put between them the widest space and distance.

---

[80] St. Basil dwells rather on the sense of "beautiful" in the lxx. kalon. The Vulgate has pulchra.

[81] cf. Bion. xvi. 1: Espere, kuaneas hieron, phile, nuktos agalma, Tosson aphauroteros menas hoson exochos astron, and Milton, P.L. iv. 605: "Hesperus, that led The starry host, rode brightest."

[82] Gen. i. 4.

8. "And God called the light Day and the darkness he called Night."[83] Since the birth of the sun, the light that it diffuses in the air, when shining on our hemisphere, is day; and the shadow produced by its disappearance is night. But at that time it was not after the movement of the sun, but following this primitive light spread abroad in the air or withdrawn in a measure determined by God, that day came and was followed by night.

"And the evening and the morning were the first day."[84] Evening is then the boundary common to day and night; and in the same way morning constitutes the approach of night to day. It was to give day the privileges of seniority that Scripture put the end of the first day before that of the first night, because night follows day: for, before the creation of light, the world was not in night, but in darkness. It is the opposite of day which was called night, and it did not receive its name until after day. Thus were created the evening and the morning.[85] Scripture means the space of a day and a night, and afterwards no more says day and night, but calls them both under the name of the more important: a custom which you will find throughout Scripture. Everywhere the measure of time is counted by days, without mention of nights.

---

[83] Gen. i. 5.

[84] Gen. i. 5.

[85] lxx. The Heb.=literally "And evening happened and morning happened, one day." On the unique reckoning of the day from evening to morning, see the late Dr. McCaul in Replies to Essays and Reviews.

"The days of our years,"[86] says the Psalmist. "Few and evil have the days of the years of my life been,"[87] said Jacob, and elsewhere "all the days of my life."[88] Thus under the form of history the law is laid down for what is to follow. And the evening and the morning were one day.[89] Why does Scripture say "one day the first day"? Before speaking to us of the second, the third, and the fourth days, would it not have been more natural to call that one the first which began the series? If it therefore says "one day," it is from a wish to determine the measure of day and night, and to combine the time that they contain. Now twenty-four hours fill up the space of one day—we mean of a day and of a night; and if, at the time of the solstices, they have not both an equal length, the time marked by Scripture does not the less circumscribe their duration. It is as though it said: twenty-four hours measure the space of a day, or that, in reality a day is the time that the heavens starting from one point take to return there. Thus, every time that, in the revolution of the sun, evening and morning occupy the world, their periodical succession never exceeds the space of one day. But must we believe in a mysterious reason for this? God who made the nature of time measured it out and determined it by intervals of days; and, wishing to give it a week as a measure, he ordered the week to revolve from period to period upon itself, to count the movement of time, forming the week of one day revolving seven times upon itself:

---

[86] Ps. xc. 10.

[87] Gen. xlvii. 9.

[88] Ps. xxiii. 6, LXX.

[89] Gen. i. 5, LXX. and Heb.

The Haxaemeron - St Basil

a proper circle begins and ends with itself. Such is also the character of eternity, to revolve upon itself and to end nowhere. If then the beginning of time is called "one day" rather than "the first day," it is because Scripture wishes to establish its relationship with eternity. It was, in reality, fit and natural to call "one" the day whose character is to be one wholly separated and isolated from all the others. If Scripture speaks to us of many ages, saying everywhere, "age of age, and ages of ages," we do not see it enumerate them as first, second, and third. It follows that we are hereby shown not so much limits, ends and succession of ages, as distinctions between various states and modes of action. "The day of the Lord," Scripture says, "is great and very terrible,"[90] and elsewhere "Woe unto you that desire the day of the Lord: to what end is it for you? The day of the Lord is darkness and not light."[91] A day of darkness for those who are worthy of darkness. No; this day without evening, without succession and without end is not unknown to Scripture, and it is the day that the Psalmist calls the eighth day, because it is outside this time of weeks.[92] Thus whether you call it day, or whether you call it eternity, you express the same idea. Give this state the name of day; there are not several, but only one. If you call it eternity still it is unique and not manifold. Thus it is in order that you may carry your thoughts forward towards a future life, that Scripture marks by the word "one" the day which

---

[90] Joel ii. 11.

[91] Amos v. 18.

[92] The argument here is due to a misapprehension of the meaning of the term eighth in Psalm vi. and xi. title. cf. n. on De Sp. S. S: 66.

is the type of eternity, the first fruits of days, the contemporary of light, the holy Lord's day honoured by the Resurrection of our Lord. And the evening and the morning were one day."

But, whilst I am conversing with you about the first evening of the world, evening takes me by surprise, and puts an end to my discourse. May the Father of the true light, Who has adorned day with celestial light, Who has made the fire to shine which illuminates us during the night, Who reserves for us in the peace of a future age a spiritual and everlasting light, enlighten your hearts in the knowledge of truth, keep you from stumbling, and grant that "you may walk honestly as in the day."[93] Thus shall you shine as the sun in the midst of the glory of the saints, and I shall glory in you in the day of Christ, to Whom belong all glory and power for ever and ever. Amen.

---

[93] Rom. xiii. 13.

Homily III

On the Firmament.

1. We have now recounted the works of the first day, or rather of one day. Far be it from me indeed, to take from it the privilege it enjoys of having been for the Creator a day apart, a day which is not counted in the same order as the others. Our discussion yesterday treated of the works of this day, and divided the narrative so as to give you food for your souls in the morning, and joy in the evening. To-day we pass on to the wonders of the second day. And here I do not wish to speak of the narrator's talent, but of the grace of Scripture, for the narrative is so naturally told that it pleases and delights all the friends of truth. It is this charm of truth which the Psalmist expresses so emphatically when he says, "How sweet are thy words unto my taste, yea, sweeter than honey to my mouth."[94] Yesterday then, as far as we were able, we delighted our souls by conversing about the oracles of God, and now to-day we are met together again on the second day to contemplate the wonders of the second day.

I know that many artisans, belonging to mechanical trades, are crowding around me. A day's labour hardly suffices to maintain them; therefore I am compelled to abridge my discourse, so as not to keep them too long from their work. What shall I say to them? The time which you lend to God is not lost: he will return it to you with large interest. Whatever difficulties may

---

[94] Ps. cxix. 103.

trouble you the Lord will disperse them. To those who have preferred spiritual welfare, He will give health of body, keenness of mind, success in business, and unbroken prosperity. And, even if in this life our efforts should not realise our hopes, the teachings of the Holy Spirit are none the less a rich treasure for the ages to come. Deliver your heart, then, from the cares of this life and give close heed to my words. Of what avail will it be to you if you are here in the body, and your heart is anxious about your earthly treasure?

2. And God said "Let there be a firmament in the midst of the waters, and let it divide the waters from the waters."[95] Yesterday we heard God's decree, "Let there be light." To-day it is, "Let there be a firmament." There appears to be something more in this. The word is not limited to a simple command. It lays down the reason necessitating the structure of the firmament: it is, it is said, to separate the waters from the waters. And first let us ask how God speaks? Is it in our manner? Does His intelligence receive an impression from objects, and, after having conceived them, make them known by particular signs appropriate to each of them? Has He consequently recourse to the organs of voice to convey His thoughts? Is He obliged to strike the air by the articulate movements of the voice, to unveil the thought hidden in His heart? Would it not seem like an idle fable to say that God should need such a circuitous method to manifest His thoughts? And is it not more conformable with true religion to say, that the divine will and the first impetus of divine intelligence are the Word of God? It is He whom

---

[95] Gen. i. 6.

Scripture vaguely represents, to show us that God has not only wished to create the world, but to create it with the help of a co-operator. Scripture might continue the history as it is begun: In the beginning God created the heaven and the earth; afterwards He created light, then He created the firmament. But, by making God command and speak, the Scripture tacitly shows us Him to Whom this order and these words are addressed. [96] It is not that it grudges us the knowledge of the truth, but that it may kindle our desire by showing us some trace and indication of the mystery. We seize with delight, and carefully keep, the fruit of laborious efforts, whilst a possession easily attained is despised.[97] Such is the road and the course which Scripture follows to lead us to the idea of the Only begotten. And certainly, God's immaterial nature had no need of the material language of voice, since His very thoughts could be transmitted to His fellow-worker. What need then of speech, for those Who by thought alone could communicate their counsels to each other? Voice was made for hearing, and hearing for voice. Where there is neither air, nor tongue, nor ear, nor that winding canal which carries sounds to the seat of sensation in the head, there is no need for words: thoughts of the soul are sufficient to transmit the will. As I said then, this language is only a wise and ingenious contrivance to set our

---

[96] Origen, c. Cels. vi. says ton men prosecheis demiourgon einai ton hui& 232;n tou Theou logon, kai hosperei autourgon tou kosmou, ton de patera tou logou, to prostetachenai to hui& 242; heautou logo poiesai ton kosmon, einai protos demiourgon. cf. Athan., c. gentes S: 48, sq.

[97] Solon is credited with the saying, duskola ta kala. cf. the German proverb, Gut ding wil weile haben, and Virgil in Georg. i. 121: "Pater ipse colendi Haud facilem esse viam voluit."

The Haxaemeron - St Basil

minds seeking the Person to whom the words are addressed.

3. In the second place, does the firmament that is called heaven differ from the firmament that God made in the beginning? Are there two heavens? The philosophers, who discuss heaven, would rather lose their tongues than grant this. There is only one heaven,[98] they pretend; and it is of a nature neither to admit of a second, nor of a third, nor of several others. The essence of the celestial body quite complete constitutes its vast unity. Because, they say, every body which has a circular motion is one and finite. And if this body is used in the construction of the first heaven, there will be nothing left for the creation of a second or a third. Here we see what those imagine who put under the Creator's hand uncreated matter; a lie that follows from the first fable. But we ask the Greek sages not to mock us before they are agreed among themselves. Because there are among them some who say there are infinite heavens and worlds.[99] When grave demonstrations

---

[98] Plato said one. poteron o& 202;n orthos hena ouranou proeirekamen; e pollous e apeirous legein en orthoteron; eiper kata to paradeigma dedemiourgemenos estai, to gar periechon panta hoposa noeta zoa, meth' heteron deuteron ouk an pot' eie...heis hode monogenes ouranos gegonos esti te kai estai. Plat., Tim. S: 11. On the other hand, was the Epicurean doctrine of the apeiria kosmon, referred to in Luc. i. 73: Ergo vivida vis animi pervicit, et extra Processit longe flammantia moenia mundi.

[99] So Anaximander (Diog. Laert. ii. 1, 2) and Democritus (Diog. Laert. ix. 44). But, as Fialon points out, the Greek philosophers used kosmos and ouranos as convertible terms: Basil uses ouranos of the firmament or sky.

shall have upset their foolish system, when the laws of geometry shall have established that, according to the nature of heaven, it is impossible that there should be two, we shall only laugh the more at this elaborate scientific trifling. These learned men see not merely one bubble but several bubbles formed by the same cause, and they doubt the power of creative wisdom to bring several heavens into being! We find, however, if we raise our eyes towards the omnipotence of God, that the strength and grandeur of the heavens differ from the drops of water bubbling on the surface of a fountain. How ridiculous, then, is their argument of impossibility! As for myself, far from not believing in a second, I seek for the third whereon the blessed Paul was found worthy to gaze.[100] And does not the Psalmist in saying "heaven of heavens"[101] give us an idea of their plurality? Is the plurality of heaven stranger than the seven circles through which nearly all the philosophers agree that the seven planets pass,–circles which they represent to us as placed in connection with each other like casks fitting the one into the other? These circles, they say, carried away in a direction contrary to that of the world, and striking the aether, make sweet and harmonious sounds,

---

[100] cf. 2 Cor. xii. 2.

[101] Ps. cxlvii. 4.

The Haxaemeron - St Basil

unequalled by the sweetest melody.[102] And if we ask them for the witness of the senses, what do they say? That we, accustomed to this noise from our birth, on account of hearing it always, have lost the sense of it; like men in smithies with their ears incessantly dinned. If I refuted this ingenious frivolity, the untruth of which is evident from the first word, it would seem as though I did not know the value of time, and mistrusted the intelligence of such an audience.

But let me leave the vanity of outsiders to those who are without, and return to the theme proper to the Church. If we believe some of those who have preceded us, we have not here the creation of a new heaven, but a new account of the first. The reason they give is, that the earlier narrative briefly described the creation of heaven and earth; while here scripture relates in greater detail the manner in which each was

---

[102] "You must conceive it" (the whirl) "to be of such a kind as this: as if in some great hollow whirl, carved throughout, there was such another, but lesser, within it, adapted to it, like casks fitted one within another; and in the same manner a third, and a fourth, and four others, for that the whirls were eight in all, as circles one within another...and that in each of its circles there was seated a siren on the upper side, carried round, and uttering one voice variegated by diverse modulations; but that the whole of them, being eight, composed one harmony." (Plat., Rep. x. 14, Davies' Trans.) Plato describes the Fates "singing to the harmony of the Sirens." Id. On the Pythagorean Music of the Spheres, cf. also Cic., De Divin. i. 3, and Macrobius In Somn: Scip. cf. Shaksp., M. of Ven. v. 1: "There's not the smallest orb which thou behold'st But in his motion like an angel sings, Still quiring to the young-eyed cherubim." And Milton, Arcades: "Then listen I To the celestial Sirens' harmony, That sit upon the nine infolded spheres, And sing to those that hold the vital sheres, And turn the adamantine spindle round On which the fate of gods and men is wound.

created. I, however, since Scripture gives to this second heaven another name and its own function, maintain that it is different from the heaven which was made at the beginning; that it is of a stronger nature and of an especial use to the universe.

4. "And God said, let there be a firmament in the midst of the waters, and let it divide the waters from the waters. And God made the firmament, and divided the waters which were under the firmament from the waters which were above the firmament."[103] Before laying hold of the meaning of Scripture let us try to meet objections from other quarters. We are asked how, if the firmament is a spherical body, as it appears to the eye, its convex circumference can contain the water which flows and circulates in higher regions? What shall we answer? One thing only: because the interior of a body presents a perfect concavity it does not necessarily follow that its exterior surface is spherical and smoothly rounded. Look at the stone vaults of baths, and the structure of buildings of cave form; the dome, which forms the interior, does not prevent the roof from having ordinarily a flat surface. Let these unfortunate men cease, then, from tormenting us and themselves about the impossibility of our retaining water in the higher regions.

Now we must say something about the nature of the firmament, and why it received the order to hold the middle place between the waters. Scripture constantly makes use of the word firmament to express extraordinary strength. "The Lord my firmament and

---

[103] Gen. i. 6, 7.

The Haxaemeron - St Basil

refuge."[104] "I have strengthened the pillars of it."[105] "Praise him in the firmament of his power."[106] The heathen writers thus call a strong body one which is compact and full,[107] to distinguish it from the mathematical body. A mathematical body is a body which exists only in the three dimensions, breadth, depth, and height. A firm body, on the contrary, adds resistance to the dimensions. It is the custom of Scripture to call firmament all that is strong and unyielding. It even uses the word to denote the condensation of the air: He, it says, who strengthens the thunder. [108] Scripture means by the strengthening of the thunder, the strength and resistance of the wind, which, enclosed in the hollows of the clouds, produces the noise of thunder when it breaks through with violence.[109] Here then, according to me, is a firm substance, capable of retaining the fluid and unstable element water; and as, according to the common acceptation, it appears that the firmament owes its origin to water, we must not believe that it resembles frozen water or any other matter produced by the filtration of water; as, for example, rock crystal, which

---

[104] Ps. xviii. 2, LXX.

[105] Ps. lxxv. 3, LXX.

[106] Ps. cl. 1. LXX.

[107] nastos (fr. nasso, press or knead)=close, firm. Democritus used it as opposed to kenon, void. Arist. fr. 202.

[108] Amos iv. 13, LXX.

[109] Pliny (Hist. Nat. ii. 43) writes: "Si in nube luctetur flatus aut vapor, tonitrua edi: si erumpat ardens, fulmina; si longiore tractu nitatur, fulgetra. His findi nubem, illis perrumpi. Etesse tonitrua impactorum ignium plagas." cf. Sen., Quaest. Nat. ii. 12.

is said to owe its metamorphosis to excessive congelation,[110] or the transparent stone [111] which forms in mines.[112] This pellucid stone, if one finds it in its natural perfection, without cracks inside, or the least spot of corruption, almost rivals the air in clearness. We cannot compare the firmament to one of these substances. To hold such an opinion about celestial bodies would be childish and foolish; and although everything may be in everything, fire in earth, air in water, and of the other elements the one in the other; although none of those which come under our senses are pure and without mixture, either with the element which serves as a medium for it, or with that which is contrary to it; I, nevertheless, dare not affirm that the firmament was formed of one of these simple substances, or of a mixture of them, for I am taught by Scripture not to allow my imagination to wander too far afield. But do not let us forget to remark that, after these divine words "let there be a firmament," it is not said "and the firmament was made" but, "and God made the firmament, and

---

[110] 'Empedokles steremnion einai ton ouranon ex a& 153;ros sumpagentos hupo puros krustalloeidos, to purodes kai aerodes en hekatero ton hemisphairion periechonta. (Plutarch peri ton areskonton tois philosophois, ii. 11.) Pliny (Hist. Nat. xxxvii. 9) says that crystal is made "gelu (vide Sir T. Browne, Vulgar Errors, ii. 1) vehementiore concreto...glaciem que esso certum est; unde et nomen graeci dedere." So Seneca, Quaest. Nat. iii. 25. Diodorus Siculus, however, asserts it "coalescere non a frigore sed divini ignis potentia." (Bibl. ii. 134.)

[111] i.e. the "Lapis Specularis," or mica, which was used for glazing windows. cf. Plin., Ep. ii. 17, and Juv., Sat. iv. 21.

[112] Mica is found in large plates in Siberia, Peru, and Mexico, as well as in Sweden and Norway.

The Haxaemeron - St Basil

divided the waters."[113] Hear, O ye deaf! See, O ye blind!–who, then, is deaf? He who does not hear this startling voice of the Holy Spirit. Who is blind? He who does not see such clear proofs of the Only begotten.[114] "Let there be a firmament." It is the voice of the primary and principal Cause. "And God made the firmament." Here is a witness to the active and creative power of God.

5. But let us continue our explanation: "Let it divide the waters from the waters."[115] The mass of waters, which from all directions flowed over the earth, and was suspended in the air, was infinite, so that there was no proportion between it and the other elements. Thus, as it has been already said, the abyss covered the earth. We give the reason for this abundance of water. None of you assuredly will attack our opinion; not even those who have the most cultivated minds, and whose piercing eye can penetrate this perishable and fleeting nature; you will not accuse me of advancing impossible or imaginary theories, nor will you ask me upon what foundation the fluid element rests. By the same reason which makes them attract the earth, heavier than water, from the extremities of the world to suspend it in the centre, they will grant us without doubt that it is due both to its natural attraction downwards and its general equilibrium, that this immense quantity of water rests motionless upon the

---

[113] Gen. i. 7.

[114] With Christian associations it is startling to read at the end of the Timaeus that the Cosmos is the eikon tou Theou, or, according to another reading, itself Theos,... monogenes on.

[115] Gen. i. 6.

earth.[116] Therefore the prodigious mass of waters was spread around the earth; not in proportion with it and infinitely larger, thanks to the foresight of the supreme Artificer, Who, from the beginning, foresaw what was to come, and at the first provided all for the future needs of the world. But what need was there for this superabundance of water? The essence of fire is necessary for the world, not only in the economy of earthly produce, but for the completion of the universe; for it would be imperfect[117] if the most powerful and the most vital of its elements were lacking.[118] Now fire and water are hostile to and destructive of each other. Fire, if it is the stronger, destroys water, and water, if in greater abundance, destroys fire. As, therefore, it was necessary to avoid an open struggle between these elements, so as not to bring about the dissolution of the universe by the total disappearance of one or the other, the sovereign Disposer created such a quantity of water that in spite of constant diminution from the effects of fire, it could last until the time fixed for the destruction of the world. He who planned all with weight and measure, He who, according to the word of Job, knows the number

---

[116] According to Plutarch (peri ton aresk: etc. iii. 10) Thales and the Stoics affirmed the earth to be spherical, Thales (id. 11) placing it "in the middle." Pliny, Hist. Nat. ii. 4, says that the earth "universi cardine stare pendentem librantem per quae pendeat; ita solam immobilem circa eam volubili universitate, eandem ex omnibus necti, eidemque omnia inniti."

[117] On kolobos, docked, curtailed, cf. Matt. xxiv. 22.

[118] The supremacy of fire was the idea of Heraclitus. To pur Theon hupeilephasin Ippasos ...kai Erakleitos. Clem. Alex., Protrep. v. 55. Plutarch has an essay on the comparative use fulness of fire and water.

The Haxaemeron - St Basil

of the drops of rain,[119] knew how long His work would last, and for how much consumption of fire He ought to allow. This is the reason of the abundance of water at the creation. Further, there is no one so strange to life as to need to learn the reason why fire is essential to the world. Not only all the arts which support life, the art of weaving, that of shoemaking, of architecture, of agriculture, have need of the help of fire, but the vegetation of trees, the ripening of fruits, the breeding of land and water animals, and their nourishment, all existed from heat from the beginning, and have been since maintained by the action of heat. The creation of heat was then indispensable for the formation and the preservation of beings, and the abundance of waters was no less so in the presence of the constant and inevitable consumption by fire.

6. Survey creation; you will see the power of heat reigning over all that is born and perishes. On account of it comes all the water spread over the earth, as well as that which is beyond our sight and is dispersed in the depths of the earth. On account of it are abundance of fountains, springs or wells, courses of rivers, both mountain torrents and ever flowing streams, for the storing of moisture in many and various reservoirs. From the East, from the winter solstice flows the Indus, the greatest river of the earth, according to geographers. From the middle of the East proceed the Bactrus,[120] the Choaspes,[121] and

---

[119] Job xxxvi. 27, LXX.

[120] Balkh.

[121] Kerak.

The Haxaemeron - St Basil

the Araxes,[122] from which the Tanais [123] detaches itself to fall into the Palus-Maeotis. [124] Add to these the Phasis [125] which descends from Mount Caucasus, and countless other rivers, which, from northern regions, flow into the Euxine Sea. From the warm countries of the West, from the foot of the Pyrenees, arise the Tartessus [126] and the Ister, [127] of which the one discharges itself into the sea beyond the Pillars and the other, after flowing through Europe, falls into Euxine Sea. Is there any need to enumerate those which the Ripaean mountains[128] pour forth in the heart of Scythia, the Rhone, [129] and so many other rivers, all navigable, which after having watered the countries of the western Gauls and of Celts and of the neighbouring barbarians, flow into the Western sea? And others from the higher regions of the South flow through Ethiopia, to discharge themselves some into our sea, others into inaccessible seas, the AEgon [130]

---

[122] Probably the Volga is meant.

[123] Don.

[124] Sea of Asov.

[125] Phaz.

[126] Ebro.

[127] The Danube.

[128] Used vaguely for any mountains in the north of Europe and Asia. Strabo (vii. pp. 295, 299) considers them fabulous.

[129] A varia lectio is Eridanus.

[130] Aigon is properly the AEgean Sea.

The Haxaemeron - St Basil

the Nyses, the Chremetes,[131] and above all the Nile, which is not of the character of a river when, like a sea, it inundates Egypt. Thus the habitable part of our earth is surrounded by water, linked together by vast seas and irrigated by countless perennial rivers, thanks to the ineffable wisdom of Him Who ordered all to prevent this rival element to fire from being entirely destroyed.

However, a time will come, when all shall be consumed by fire; as Isaiah says of the God of the universe in these words, "That saith to the deep, Be dry, and I will dry up thy rivers." [132] Reject then the foolish wisdom of this world, [133] and receive with me the more simple but infallible doctrine of truth.

7. Therefore we read: "Let there be a firmament in the midst of the waters, and let it divide the waters from the waters." I have said what the word firmament in Scripture means. It is not in reality a firm and solid substance which has weight and resistance; this name would otherwise have better suited the earth.

---

[131] Basil's geography is bad. He might have improved it by consulting Strabo or Ptolemaeus, but has been content to go for his facts to Aristotle (Met. i. 13), whose errors he repeats. Fialon remarks "nouvelle preuve de l'indifference des cites grecques de l' Asie pour cet Occident lointain dont elles se separerent si facilement." If this refers to the theological separation it is hardly fair. The East in the 4th c. and 5th c. shewed no indifference to the sympathy of the W., and when the split came the "separation" was not taken "easily."

[132] Isa. xliv. 27.

[133] Schools of "the wisdom of the world" did, however, teach that the world was a world genomenon kai phtharton. cf. Lucretius v. 322, "totum nativum mortali corpore constat."

The Haxaemeron - St Basil

But, as the substance of superincumbent bodies is light, without consistency, and cannot be grasped by any one of our senses, it is in comparison with these pure and imperceptible substances that the firmament has received its name. Imagine a place fit to divide the moisture, sending it, if pure and filtered, into higher regions, and making it fall, if it is dense and earthy; to the end that by the gradual withdrawal of the moist particles the same temperature may be preserved from the beginning to the end. You do not believe in this prodigious quantity of water; but you do not take into account the prodigious quantity of heat, less considerable no doubt in bulk, but exceedingly powerful nevertheless, if you consider it as destructive of moisture. It attracts surrounding moisture, as the melon shows us, and consumes it as quickly when attracted, as the flame of the lamp draws to it the fuel supplied by the wick and burns it up. Who doubts that the aether is an ardent fire? [134] If an impassable limit had not been assigned to it by the Creator, what would prevent it from setting on fire and consuming all that is near it, and absorbing all the moisture from existing things? The aerial waters which veil the heavens with vapours that are sent forth by rivers, fountains, marshes, lakes, and seas, prevent the aether from invading and burning up the universe. Thus we see even this sun, in the summer season, dry up in a moment a damp and marshy country, and make it perfectly arid. What has become of all the water? Let these masters of omniscience tell us. Is it

---

[134] So the "liquidissimus aether" of the Epicurean Lucretius (v. 501), "Suos ignes fert;" i.e. the fiery stars are of the nature of the element in which they move. cf. the Stoic Manilius i. 149, "Ignis in aethereas volucer se sustulit oras summaque complexus stellantis culmina coeli, Flammarum vallo naturae moenia fecit."

The Haxaemeron - St Basil

not plain to every one that it has risen in vapour, and has been consumed by the heat of the sun? They say, none the less, that even the sun is without heat. What time they lose in words! And see what proof they lean upon to resist what is perfectly plain. Its colour is white, and neither reddish nor yellow. It is not then fiery by nature, and its heat results, they say, from the velocity of its rotation. [135] What do they gain? That the sun does not seem to absorb moisture? I do not, however, reject this statement, although it is false, because it helps my argument. I said that the consumption of heat required this prodigious quantity of water. That the sun owes its heat to its nature, or that heat results from its action, makes no difference, provided that it produces the same effects upon the same matter. If you kindle fire by rubbing two pieces of wood together, or if you light them by holding them to a flame, you will have absolutely the same effect. Besides, we see that the great wisdom of Him who governs all, makes the sun travel from one region to another, for fear that, if it remained always in the same place, its excessive heat would destroy the order of the universe. Now it passes into southern regions about the time of the winter solstice, now it returns to the sign of the equinox; from thence it betakes itself to northern regions during the summer solstice, and keeps up by this imperceptible passage a pleasant temperature throughout all the world.

---

[135] So Aristotle, Meteor. i. 3, 30. Oromen de ten kinesin hoti dunatai diakrinein ton a& 153;ra kai ekpuroun hoste kai ta pheromena tekomena phainesthai pollakis. To men oun gignesthai ten alean kai ten thermoteta hikane esti paraskeuazein kai he tou heliou phora monon.

The Haxaemeron - St Basil

Let the learned people see if they do not disagree among themselves. The water which the sun consumes is, they say, what prevents the sea from rising and flooding the rivers; the warmth of the sun leaves behind the salts and the bitterness of the waters, and absorbs from them the pure and drinkable particles, [136] thanks to the singular virtue of this planet in attracting all that is light and in allowing to fall, like mud and sediment, all which is thick and earthy. From thence come the bitterness, the salt taste and the power of withering and drying up which are characteristic of the sea. While as is notorious, they hold these views, they shift their ground and say that moisture cannot be lessened by the sun.[137]

8. "And God called the firmament heaven."[138] The nature of right belongs to another, and the firmament only shares it on account of its resemblance to heaven. We often find the visible region called

---

[136] cf. Diog. Laert. vii. on Zeno. Trepesthai de ta empura tauta kai ta alla astra, ton men helion ek tes megales thalattes. So Zeno, Chrysippus, and Posidonius.

[137] Pliny (ii. 103, 104) writes: "Itaque solis ardore siccatur liquor; ...sic mari late patenti saporem incoqui salis, aut quia exhausto inde dulci tenuique, quod facillime, trahat vis ignea, omne asperius crassiusque linquatur: ideo summa aequarum aqua dulciorem profundam: hanc esse veriorem causam asperi saporis, quam quod mare terrae sudor sit aeternus: aut quia plurimum ex arido misceatur illi vapore, aut quia terrae natura sicut medicatas aquas inficiat." The first of these three theories was that of Hippocrates (De Aere, Locis, et Aquis, iv. 197) and of Anaximander (Plutarch peri ton aresk, etc. ii. 552). On the second vide Arist., Prob. xxiii. 30. The idea of the sea being the earth's sweat was that of Empedocles. cf. Arist., Meteor. ii. 1.

[138] Gen. i. 8.

The Haxaemeron - St Basil

heaven, on account of the density and continuity of the air within our ken, and deriving its name "heaven" from the word which means to see.[139] It is of it that Scripture says, "The fowl of the air," [140] "Fowl that may fly...in the open firmament of heaven;" [141] and, elsewhere, "They mount up to heaven." [142] Moses, blessing the tribe of Joseph, desires for it the fruits and the dews of heaven, of the suns of summer and the conjunctions of the moon, and blessings from the tops of the mountains and from the everlasting hills,[143] in one word, from all which fertilises the earth. In the curses on Israel it is said, "And thy heaven that is over thy head shall be brass." [144] What does this mean? It threatens him with a complete drought, with an absence of the aerial waters which cause the fruits of the earth to be brought forth and to grow.

Since, then, Scripture says that the dew or the rain falls from heaven, we understand that it is from those waters which have been ordered to occupy the higher regions. When the exhalations from the earth, gathered together in the heights of the air, are condensed under the pressure of the wind, this aerial

---

[139] The derivation of ouranos from horao is imaginary. Aristotle (De Coel i. 19, 9) derives it from horos, a boundary. cf. Orizon. The real root is the Skt. var=cover. M. Mueller, Oxford Essays, 1856.

[140] Ps. viii. 8.

[141] Gen. i. 20.

[142] Ps. cvii. 26.

[143] cf. Deut. xxxiii. 13-15, LXX.

[144] Deut. xxviii. 23.

The Haxaemeron - St Basil

moisture diffuses itself in vaporous and light clouds; then mingling again, it forms drops which fall, dragged down by their own weight; and this is the origin of rain. When water beaten by the violence of the wind, changes into foam, and passing through excessive cold quite freezes, it breaks the cloud, and falls as snow.[145] You can thus account for all the moist substances that the air suspends over our heads.

And do not let any one compare with the inquisitive discussions of philosophers upon the heavens, the simple and inartificial character of the utterances of the Spirit; as the beauty of chaste women surpasses that of a harlot,[146] so our arguments are superior to those of our opponents. They only seek to persuade by forced reasoning. With us truth presents itself naked and without artifice. But why torment ourselves to refute the errors of philosophers, when it is sufficient to produce their mutually contradictory books, and, as quiet spectators, to watch the war?[147] For those thinkers are not less numerous, nor less celebrated, nor more sober in speech in fighting their adversaries, who say that the universe is being consumed by fire, and that from the seeds which remain in the ashes of the burnt world all is being brought to life again. Hence in the world there is

---

[145] cf. Arist., Meteor. i. 9-12, Plutarch peri ton aresk. etc. iii. 4.

[146] Fialon quotes Hor., Ep. i. 18: "Ut matrona meretrici dispar erit atque Discolor."

[147] The well known "Per campos instructa, tua sine parte pericli suave etiam belli certamina magna tueri" (Lucr. ii. 5) may be an echo of some Greek lines in the preacher's mind, just as the preceding "suave mari magno" is of Menander.

destruction and palingenesis to infinity. [148] All, equally far from the truth, find each on their side by-ways which lead them to error.

9. But as far as concerns the separation of the waters I am obliged to contest the opinion of certain writers in the Church[149] who, under the shadow of high and sublime conceptions, have launched out into metaphor, and have only seen in the waters a figure to denote spiritual and incorporeal powers. In the higher regions, above the firmament, dwell the better; in the lower regions, earth and matter are the dwelling place of the malignant. So, say they, God is praised by the waters that are above the heaven, that is to say, by the good powers, the purity of whose soul makes them worthy to sing the praises of God. And the waters which are under the heaven represent the wicked spirits, who from their natural height have fallen into the abyss of evil. Turbulent, seditious, agitated by the tumultuous waves of passion, they have received the name of sea, because of the instability and the inconstancy of their movements. [150] Let us reject these theories as dreams and old women's tales. Let us understand that by water water is meant; for the dividing of the waters by the firmament let us accept the reason which has been

---

[148] These Stoical atheists did also agree with the generality of the other Stoical theists in supposing a successive infinity of worlds generated and corrupted" (apeiria kosmon) "by reason of intervening periodical conflagrations." Cudworth, I. iii. 23.

[149] i.e. Origen.

[150] cf. Jerome to Pammachius against John of Jerusalem, S: 7 (in this edition vol. vi. p. 428) and Origen's Homily on Genesis, preserved in the Translation of Rufinus.

given us. Although, however, waters above the heaven are invited to give glory to the Lord of the Universe, do not let us think of them as intelligent beings; the heavens are not alive because they "declare the glory of God," nor the firmament a sensible being because it "sheweth His handiwork." [151] And if they tell you that the heavens mean contemplative powers, and the firmament active powers which produce good, we admire the theory as ingenious without being able to acknowledge the truth of it. For thus dew, the frost, cold and heat, which in Daniel are ordered to praise the Creator of all things, [152] will be intelligent and invisible natures. But this is only a figure, accepted as such by enlightened minds, to complete the glory of the Creator. Besides, the waters above the heavens, these waters privileged by the virtue which they possess in themselves, are not the only waters to celebrate the praises of God. "Praise the Lord from the earth, ye dragons and all deeps." [153] Thus the singer of the Psalms does not reject the deeps which our inventors of allegories rank in the divisions of evil; he admits them to the universal choir of creation, and the deeps sing in their language a harmonious hymn to the glory of the Creator.

10. "And God saw that it was good." God does not judge of the beauty of His work by the charm of the eyes, and He does not form the same idea of beauty that we do. What He esteems beautiful is that which

---

[151] Ps. xviii. 1.

[152] Bened.

[153] Ps. cxlviii. 7.

The Haxaemeron - St Basil

presents in its perfection all the fitness[154] of art, and that which tends to the usefulness of its end. He, then, who proposed to Himself a manifest design in His works, approved each one of them, as fulfilling its end in accordance with His creative purpose. A hand, an eye, or any portion of a statue lying apart from the rest, would look beautiful to no one. But if each be restored to its own place, the beauty of proportion, until now almost unperceived, would strike even the most uncultivated. But the artist, before uniting the parts of his work, distinguishes and recognises the beauty of each of them, thinking of the object that he has in view. It is thus that Scripture depicts to us the Supreme Artist, praising each one of His works; soon, when His work is complete, He will accord well deserved praise to the whole together. Let me here end my discourse on the second day, to allow my industrious hearers to examine what they have just heard. May their memory retain it for the profit of their soul; may they by careful meditation inwardly digest and benefit by what I say. As for those who live by their work, let me allow them to attend all day to their

---

[154] kalon men oun estin ho an d' hauto haireton on epaineton e, ho an agathon on hedu e hoti agathon. Arist., Rhet. i. 9. cf. E. Burke (On the Sublime and Beautiful, iii. S: 6): "It is true that the infinitely wise and good creator has, of his bounty, frequently joined beauty to those things which he has made useful to us. But this does not prove that our idea of use and beauty are the same thing, or that they are in any way dependent on each other." Dr. Johnson instances a painting on a coffee-cup as beautiful, but not useful. "Boswell," Ann. 1772. St. Basil's idea is in accord with that of Ruskin (Mod. P. chap. vi.). "In all high ideas of beauty it is more than probable that much of the pleasure depends on delicate and untraceable perception of fitness, propriety, and relation, which are purely intellectual, and through which we arrive at our noblest ideas of what is commonly and rightly called intellectual beauty.'"

business, so that they may come, with a soul free from anxiety, to the banquet of my discourse in the evening. May God who, after having made such great things, put such weak words in my mouth, grant you the intelligence of His truth, so that you may raise yourselves from visible things to the invisible Being, and that the grandeur and beauty of creatures may give you a just idea of the Creator. For the visible things of Him from the creation of the world are clearly seen, and His power and divinity are eternal.[155] Thus earth, air, sky, water, day, night, all visible things, remind us of who is our Benefactor. We shall not therefore give occasion to sin, we shall not give place to the enemy within us, if by unbroken recollection we keep God ever dwelling in our hearts, to Whom be all glory and all adoration, now and for ever, world without end. Amen.

---

[155] cf. Rom. i. 20.

The Haxaemeron - St Basil

Homily IV

Upon the gathering together of the waters.

1. There are towns where the inhabitants, from dawn to eve, feast their eyes on the tricks of innumerable conjurors. They are never tired of hearing dissolute songs which cause much impurity to spring up in their souls, and they are often called happy, because they neglect the cares of business and trades useful to life, and pass the time, which is assigned to them on this earth, in idleness and pleasure. They do not know that a theatre full of impure sights is, for those who sit there, a common school of vice; that these melodious and meretricious songs insinuate themselves into men's souls, and all who hear them, eager to imitate the notes [156] of harpers and pipers, are filled with filthiness. [157] Some others, who are wild after horses, think they are backing their horses in their dreams; they harness their chariots, change their drivers, and even in sleep are not free from the folly of the day. [158] And shall we, whom the Lord, the great worker of

---

[156] krouma, properly "beat," "stroke," is used of the blow of the plectrum on the string, and hence of the note produced.

[157] cf. Plato, Rep. iii. 18, ad init., and his reference to the malthakos aichmetes of Homer, Il. xvii. 586. The same subject is treated of the Laws ii. S: 3 and 5 and vii.

[158] cf. Ar., Nub. 16, oneiropolei hippous and 27, oneiropolei kai katheudon hippiken. So Claudian, De vi. Cons. Hon. 1, sq.: Omnia quae sensu volvuntur vota diurno, Pectore sopito reddit amica quies. Venator defessa toro cum membra reponit, Mens tamen ad sylvas et sua lustra redit. Judicibus lites, aurigae somnia currus, Vanaque nocturnis meta cavetur equis.

marvels, calls to the contemplation of His own works, tire of looking at them, or be slow to hear the words of the Holy Spirit? Shall we not rather stand around the vast and varied workshop of divine creation and, carried back in mind to the times of old, shall we not view all the order of creation? Heaven, poised like a dome, to quote the words of the prophet; [159] earth, this immense mass which rests upon itself; the air around it, of a soft and fluid nature, a true and continual nourishment for all who breathe it, of such tenuity that it yields and opens at the least movement of the body, opposing no resistance to our motions, while, in a moment, it streams back to its place, behind those who cleave it; water, finally, that supplies drink for man, or may be designed for our other needs, and the marvellous gathering together of it into definite places which have been assigned to it: such is the spectacle which the words which I have just read will show you.

2. "And God said, Let the waters under the heaven be gathered together unto one place, and let the dry land appear, and it was so." And the water which was under the heaven gathered together unto one place; "And God called the dry land earth and the gathering together of the waters called He seas." [160] What trouble you have given me in my previous discourses by asking me why the earth was invisible, why all bodies are naturally endued with colour, and why all colour comes under the sense of sight. And, perhaps, my reason did not appear sufficient to you, when I said that the earth, without being naturally invisible,

---

[159] Isa. xl. 22, LXX.

[160] Gen. i. 9, 10.

was so to us, because of the mass of water that entirely covered it. Hear then how Scripture explains itself. "Let the waters be gathered together, and let the dry land appear." The veil is lifted and allows the earth, hitherto invisible, to be seen. Perhaps you will ask me new questions. And first, is it not a law of nature that water flows downwards? Why, then, does Scripture refer this to the fiat of the Creator? As long as water is spread over a level surface, it does not flow; it is immovable. But when it finds any slope, immediately the foremost portion falls, then the one that follows takes its place, and that one is itself replaced by a third. Thus incessantly they flow, pressing the one on the other, and the rapidity of their course is in proportion to the mass of water that is being carried, and the declivity down which it is borne. If such is the nature of water, it was supererogatory to command it to gather into one place. It was bound, on account of its natural instability, to fall into the most hollow part of the earth and not to stop until the levelling of its surface. We see how there is nothing so level as the surface of water. Besides, they add, how did the waters receive an order to gather into one place, when we see several seas, separated from each other by the greatest distances? To the first question I reply: Since God's command, you know perfectly well the motion of water; you know that it is unsteady and unstable and falls naturally over declivities and into hollow places. But what was its nature before this command made it take its course? You do not know yourself, and you have heard from no eye-witness. Think, in reality, that a word of God makes the nature, and that this order is for the creature a direction for its future course. There was only one creation of day and night, and since that moment they have incessantly succeeded each other and divided time into equal parts.

3. "Let the waters be gathered together." It was ordered that it should be the natural property of water to flow, and in obedience to this order, the waters are never weary in their course. In speaking thus, I have only in view the flowing property of waters. Some flow of their own accord like springs and rivers, others are collected and stationary. But I speak now of flowing waters. "Let the waters be gathered together unto one place." Have you never thought, when standing near a spring which is sending forth water abundantly, Who makes this water spring from the bowels of the earth? Who forced it up? Where are the store-houses which send it forth? To what place is it hastening? How is it that it is never exhausted here, and never overflows there? All this comes from that first command; it was for the waters a signal for their course.

In all the story of the waters remember this first order, "let the waters be gathered together." To take their assigned places they were obliged to flow, and, once arrived there, to remain in their place and not to go farther. Thus in the language of Ecclesiastes, "All the waters run into the sea; yet the sea is not full." [161] Waters flow in virtue of God's order, and the sea is enclosed in limits according to this first law, "Let the waters be gathered together unto one place." For fear the water should spread beyond its bed, and in its successive invasions cover one by one all countries, and end by flooding the whole earth, it received the order to gather unto one place. Thus we often see the

---

[161] Eccl. i. 6, 7.

The Haxaemeron - St Basil

furious sea raising mighty waves to the heaven, and, when once it has touched the shore, break its impetuosity in foam and retire. "Fear ye not me, saith the Lord....which have placed the sand for the bound of the sea." [162] A grain of sand, the weakest thing possible, curbs the violence of the ocean. For what would prevent the Red Sea from invading the whole of Egypt, which lies lower, and uniting itself to the other sea which bathes its shores, were it not fettered by the fiat of the Creator? And if I say that Egypt is lower than the Red Sea, it is because experience has convinced us of it every time that an attempt has been made to join the sea of Egypt [163] to the Indian Ocean, of which the Red Sea is a part.[164] Thus we have renounced this enterprise, as also have the Egyptian

---

[162] Jer. v. 22.

[163] i.e. the Mediterranean.

[164] Geminum mare...quod Rubrum dixere nostri...in duos dividitur sinus. Is qui ab oriente Persicus est...altero sinu Arabico nominato. Plin. vi. 28.

The Haxaemeron - St Basil

Sesostris, who conceived the idea, and Darius the Mede who afterwards wished to carry it out. [165]

I report this fact to make you understand the full force of the command, "Let the waters be gathered unto one place"; that is to say, let there be no other gathering, and, once gathered, let them not disperse.

4. To say that the waters were gathered in one place indicates that previously they were scattered in many places. The mountains, intersected by deep ravines, accumulated water in their valleys, when from every direction the waters betook themselves to the one gathering place. What vast plains, in their extent resembling wide seas, what valleys, what cavities hollowed in many different ways, at that time full of water, must have been emptied by the command of God! But we must not therefore say, that if the water covered the face of the earth, all the basins which have since received the sea were originally full. Where can the gathering of the waters have come

---

[165] This illustration is taken from the work on which Basil has been so largely dependent, the Meterology of Aristotle (i. 14, 548). Pliny (vi. 33) writes: "Daneos Portus, ex quo navigabilem alveum perducere in Nilum, qua parte ad Delta dictum decurrit lxii. mill. D. Pass. intervallo, quod inter flumen et Rubrum mare inter est, primus omnium Sesostris AEgypti rex cogitavit; mox Darius Persarum; deinde Ptolemaeus sequens" (i.e. Ptolemy II.) "...deterruit inundationis metus, excelsiore tribus cubitis Rubro mari comperto quam terra AEgypti." Herodotus (ii. 158) attributes the canal to Necho. Strabo (xvii. 804) says Darius, in supposing Egypt to lie lower than the sea, was pseudei peistheis. The early canal, choked by sand, was reopened by Trajan, and choked again. Amron, Omar's general, again cleared it, but it was blocked a.d. 767. The present Suez Canal, opened in 1869, follows a new course.

The Haxaemeron - St Basil

from if the basins were already full? These basins, we reply, were only prepared at the moment when the water had to unite in a single mass. At that time the sea which is beyond Gadeira [166] and the vast ocean, so dreaded by navigators, which surrounds the isle of Britain and western Spain, did not exist. But, all of a sudden, God created this vast space, and the mass of waters flowed in.

Now if our explanation of the creation of the world may appear contrary to experience, (because it is evident that all the waters did not flow together in one place,) many answers may be made, all obvious as soon as they are stated. Perhaps it is even ridiculous to reply to such objections. Ought they to bring forward in opposition ponds and accumulations of rain water, and think that this is enough to upset our reasonings? Evidently the chief and most complete affluence of the waters was what received the name of gathering unto one place. For wells are also gathering places for water, made by the hand of man to receive the moisture diffused in the hollow of the earth. This name of gathering does not mean any chance massing of water, but the greatest and most important one, wherein the element is shewn collected together. In the same way that fire, in spite of its being divided into minute particles which are sufficient for our needs here, is spread in a mass in the aether; in the same way that air, in spite of a like minute division, has occupied the region round the earth; so also water, in spite of the small amount spread abroad everywhere, only forms one gathering together, that which separates the whole element

---

[166] i.e. Cadiz, a corruption of Gadeira, which, like Geder and Gadara, is connected with the Phoenician Gadir, an enclosure.

The Haxaemeron - St Basil

from the rest. Without doubt the lakes as well those of the northern regions and those that are to be found in Greece, in Macedonia, in Bithynia and in Palestine, are gatherings together of waters; but here it means the greatest of all, that gathering the extent of which equals that of the earth. The first contain a great quantity of water; no one will deny this. Nevertheless no one could reasonably give them the name of seas, not even if they are like the great sea, charged with salt and sand. They instance for example, the Lacus Asphaltitis in Judaea, and the Serbonian lake which extends between Egypt and Palestine in the Arabian desert. These are lakes, and there is only one sea, as those affirm who have travelled round the earth. Although some authorities think the Hyrcanian and Caspian Seas are enclosed in their own boundaries, if we are to believe the geographers, they communicate with each other and together discharge themselves into the Great Sea. [167] It is thus that, according to their account, the Red Sea and that beyond Gadeira only form one. Then why did God call the different masses of water seas? This is the reason; the waters flowed into one place, and their different accumulations, that is to say, the gulfs that the earth embraced in her folds, received from the Lord the name of seas: North Sea, South Sea, Eastern Sea, and Western Sea. The seas have even their own names, the Euxine, the Propontis, the Hellespont, the AEgean, the Ionian, the Sardinian, the Sicilian, the Tyrrhene, and many other names of which an exact enumeration would now be too long, and quite out of place. See why God calls the gathering together of waters seas. But let us

---

[167] Pliny (vi. 15) shared a common error that the Caspian flowed into a Northern Sea. The eastern part was known as the Hyrcanian, the western as the Caspian. Strabo xi. 507, et sq.

The Haxaemeron - St Basil

return to the point from which the course of my argument has diverted me.

5. And God said: "Let the waters be gathered together unto one place and let the dry land appear." He did not say let the earth appear, so as not to show itself again without form, mud-like, and in combination with the water, nor yet endued with proper form and virtue. At the same time, lest we should attribute the drying of the earth to the sun, the Creator shows it to us dried before the creation of the sun. Let us follow the thought Scripture gives us. Not only the water which was covering the earth flowed off from it, but all that which had filtered into its depths withdrew in obedience to the irresistible order of the sovereign Master. And it was so. This is quite enough to show that the Creator's voice had effect: however, in several editions, there is added "And the water which was under the heavens gathered itself unto one place and the dry land was seen;" words that other interpreters have not given, and which do not appear conformable to Hebrew usage. In fact, after the assertion, "and it was so," it is superfluous to repeat exactly the same thing. In accurate copies these words are marked with an obelus, [168] which is the sign of rejection.

---

[168] The obelus () is used by Jerome to mark superfluous matter in the lxx. cf. Jer. p. 494, in Canon Fremantle's Translation. The addition in question appears neither in the Vulgate, nor in Aquila, or Symmachus, or Theodotion. Ambrose, however, in Hexaem. iii. 5 approves of it.

"And God called the dry land earth; and the gathering together of the waters called He seas." [169] Why does Scripture say above that the waters were gathered together unto one place, and that the dry earth appeared? Why does it add here the dry land appeared, and God gave it the name of earth? It is that dryness is the property which appears to characterize the nature of the subject, whilst the word earth is only its simple name. Just as reason is the distinctive faculty of man, and the word man serves to designate the being gifted with this faculty, so dryness is the special and peculiar quality of the earth. The element essentially dry receives therefore the name of earth, as the animal who has a neigh for a characteristic cry is called a horse. The other elements, like the earth, have received some peculiar property which distinguishes them from the rest, and makes them known for what they are. Thus water has cold for its distinguishing property; air, moisture; fire, heat. But this theory really applies only to the primitive elements of the world. The elements which contribute to the formation of bodies, and come under our senses, show us these qualities in combination, and in the whole of nature our eyes and senses can find nothing which is completely singular, simple and pure. Earth is at the same time dry and cold; water, cold and moist; air, moist and warm; fire, warm and dry. It is by the combination of their qualities that the different elements can mingle. Thanks to a common quality each of them mixes with a neighbouring element, and this natural alliance attaches it to the contrary element. For example, earth, which is at the same time dry and cold, finds in cold a relationship which unites it to water, and by the means of water

---

[169] Gen. i. 10.

unites itself to air. Water placed between the two, appears to give each a hand, and, on account of its double quality, allies itself to earth by cold and to air by moisture. Air, in its turn, takes the middle place and plays the part of a mediator between the inimical natures of water and fire, united to the first by moisture, and to the second by heat. Finally fire, of a nature at the same time warm and dry, is linked to air by warmth, and by its dryness reunites itself to the earth. And from this accord and from this mutual mixture of elements, results a circle and an harmonious choir whence each of the elements deserves its name. I have said this in order to explain why God has given to the dry land the name of earth, without however calling the earth dry. It is because dryness is not one of those qualities which the earth acquired afterwards, but one of those which constituted its essence from the beginning. Now that which causes a body to exist, is naturally antecedent to its posterior qualities and has a pre-eminence over them. It is then with reason that God chose the most ancient characteristic of the earth whereby to designate it.

6. "And God saw that it was good." [170] Scripture does not merely wish to say that a pleasing aspect of the sea presented itself to God. It is not with eyes that the Creator views the beauty of His works. He contemplates them in His ineffable wisdom. A fair sight is the sea all bright in a settled calm; fair too, when, ruffled by a light breeze of wind, its surface shows tints of purple and azure,–when, instead of lashing with violence the neighbouring shores, it

---

[170] Gen. i. 10.

The Haxaemeron - St Basil

seems to kiss them with peaceful caresses. However, it is not in this that Scripture makes God find the goodness and charm of the sea. Here it is the purpose of the work which makes the goodness.

In the first place sea water is the source of all the moisture of the earth. It filters through imperceptible conduits, as is proved by the subterranean openings and caves whither its waves penetrate; it is received in oblique and sinuous canals; then, driven out by the wind, it rises to the surface of the earth, and breaks it, having become drinkable and free from its bitterness by this long percolation. Often, moved by the same cause, it springs even from mines that it has crossed, deriving warmth from them, and rises boiling, and bursts forth of a burning heat, as may be seen in islands and on the sea coast; even inland in certain places, in the neighbourhood of rivers, to compare little things with great, almost the same phenomena occur. To what do these words tend? To prove that the earth is all undermined with invisible conduits, where the water travels everywhere underground from the sources of the sea.

7. Thus, in the eyes of God, the sea is good, because it makes the under current of moisture in the depths of the earth. It is good again, because from all sides it receives the rivers without exceeding its limits. It is good, because it is the origin and source of the waters in the air. Warmed by the rays of the sun, it escapes in vapour, is attracted into the high regions of the air, and is there cooled on account of its rising high above the refraction of the rays from the ground, and, the shade of the clouds adding to this refrigeration, it is changed into rain and fattens the earth. If people are

The Haxaemeron - St Basil

incredulous, let them look at caldrons on the fire, which, though full of water, are often left empty because all the water is boiled and resolved into vapour. Sailors, too, boil even sea water, collecting the vapour in sponges, to quench their thirst in pressing need.

Finally the sea is good in the eyes of God, because it girdles the isles, of which it forms at the same time the rampart and the beauty, because it brings together the most distant parts of the earth, and facilitates the inter-communication of mariners. By this means it gives us the boon of general information, supplies the merchant with his wealth, and easily provides for the necessities of life, allowing the rich to export their superfluities, and blessing the poor with the supply of what they lack.

But whence do I perceive the goodness of the Ocean, as it appeared in the eyes of the Creator? If the Ocean is good and worthy of praise before God, how much more beautiful is the assembly of a Church like this, where the voices of men, of children, and of women, arise in our prayers to God mingling and resounding like the waves which beat upon the shore. This Church also enjoys a profound calm, and malicious spirits cannot trouble it with the breath of heresy. Deserve, then, the approbation of the Lord by remaining faithful to such good guidance, in our Lord Jesus Christ, to whom be glory and power for ever and ever. Amen.

Homily V

The Germination of the Earth.

1. "And God said Let the earth bring forth grass, the herb yielding seed, and the fruit tree yielding fruit after his kind, whose seed is in itself." [171] It was deep wisdom that commanded the earth, when it rested after discharging the weight of the waters, first to bring forth grass, then wood as we see it doing still at this time. For the voice that was then heard and this command were as a natural and permanent law for it; it gave fertility and the power to produce fruit for all ages to come; "Let the earth bring forth." The production of vegetables shows first germination. When the germs begin to sprout they form grass; this develops and becomes a plant, which insensibly receives its different articulations, and reaches its maturity in the seed. Thus all things which sprout and are green are developed. "Let the earth bring forth green grass." Let the earth bring forth by itself without having any need of help from without. Some consider the sun as the source of all productiveness on the earth. It is, they say, the action of the sun's heat which attracts the vital force from the centre of the earth to the surface. The reason why the adornment of the earth was before the sun is the following; that those who worship the sun, as the source of life, may renounce their error. If they be well persuaded that the earth was adorned before the genesis of the sun, they will retract their unbounded admiration for it, because they see grass and plants vegetate before it

---

[171] Gen. i. 11.

The Haxaemeron - St Basil

rose. [172] If then the food for the flocks was prepared, did our race appear less worthy of a like solicitude? He, who provided pasture for horses and cattle, thought before all of your riches and pleasures. If he fed your cattle, it was to provide for all the needs of your life. And what object was there in the bringing forth of grain, if not for your subsistence? Moreover, many grasses and vegetables serve for the food of man.

2. "Let the earth bring forth grass yielding seed after his kind." So that although some kind of grass is of service to animals, even their gain is our gain too, and seeds are especially designed for our use. Such is the true meaning of the words that I have quoted. "Let the earth bring forth grass, the herb yielding seed after his kind." In this manner we can re-establish the order of the words, of which the construction seems faulty in the actual version, and the economy of nature will be rigorously observed. In fact, first comes germination, then verdure, then the growth of the plant, which after having attained its full growth arrives at perfection in seed.

How then, they say, can Scripture describe all the plants of the earth as seed-bearing, when the reed, couch-grass,[173] mint, crocus, garlic, and the flowering rush and countless other species, produce no seed? To this we reply that many vegetables have their seminal virtue in the lower part and in the roots. The

---

[172] Empedocles, according to Plutarch (peri ton aresk, etc. v. 342) prota ton zoon ta dendra ek ges anadunai phesi, prin ton helion periaplothenai kai prin hemeran kai nukta diakrithenai.

[173] Triticum repens.

need, for example, after its annual growth sends forth a protuberance from its roots, which takes the place of seed for future trees. Numbers of other vegetables are the same and all over the earth reproduce by the roots. Nothing then is truer than that each plant produces its seed or contains some seminal virtue; this is what is meant by "after its kind." So that the shoot of a reed does not produce an olive tree, but from a reed grows another reed, and from one sort of seed a plant of the same sort always germinates. Thus, all which sprang from the earth, in its first bringing forth, is kept the same to our time, thanks to the constant reproduction of kind.[174]

"Let the earth bring forth." See how, at this short word, at this brief command, the cold and sterile earth travailed and hastened to bring forth its fruit, as it cast away its sad and dismal covering to clothe itself in a more brilliant robe, proud of its proper adornment and displaying the infinite variety of plants.

I want creation to penetrate you with so much admiration that everywhere, wherever you may be, the least plant may bring to you the clear remembrance of the Creator. If you see the grass of the fields, think of human nature, and remember the comparison of the wise Isaiah. "All flesh is grass, and all the goodliness thereof is as the flower of the field." Truly the rapid flow of life, the short gratification and pleasure that an instant of happiness gives a man, all wonderfully suit the comparison of the prophet. To-day he is vigorous in body, fattened by luxury, and in the

---

[174] On the history of this doctrine, of which Linnaeus was the latest great exponent, and its contradiction in Darwin, see Haeckel's Schoepfungsgeschichte, vol. i. ch. 2.

The Haxaemeron - St Basil

prime of life, with complexion fair like the flowers, strong and powerful and of irresistible energy; tomorrow and he will be an object of pity, withered by age or exhausted by sickness. Another shines in all the splendour of a brilliant fortune, and around him are a multitude of flatterers, an escort of false friends on the track of his good graces; a crowd of kinsfolk, but of no true kin; a swarm of servants who crowd after him to provide for his food and for all his needs; and in his comings and goings this innumerable suite, which he drags after him, excites the envy of all whom he meets. To fortune may be added power in the State, honours bestowed by the imperial throne, the government of a province, or the command of armies; a herald who precedes him is crying in a loud voice; lictors right and left also fill his subjects with awe, blows, confiscations, banishments, imprisonments, and all the means by which he strikes intolerable terror into all whom he has to rule. And what then? One night, a fever, a pleurisy, or an inflammation of the lungs, snatches away this man from the midst of men, stripped in a moment of all his stage accessories, and all this, his glory, is proved a mere dream. Therefore the Prophet has compared human glory to the weakest flower.

3. Up to this point, the order in which plants shoot bears witness to their first arrangement. Every herb, every plant proceeds from a germ. If, like the couch-grass and the crocus, it throws out a shoot from its root and from this lower protuberance, it must always germinate and start outwards. If it proceeds from a seed, there is still, by necessity, first a germ, then the sprout, then green foliage, and finally the fruit which ripens upon a stalk hitherto dry and thick. "Let the

earth bring forth grass." When the seed falls into the earth, which contains the right combination of heat and moisture, it swells and becomes porous, and, grasping the surrounding earth, attracts to itself all that is suitable for it and that has affinity to it. These particles of earth, however small they may be, as they fall and insinuate themselves into all the pores of the seed, broaden its bulk and make it send forth roots below, and shoot upwards, sending forth stalks no less numerous than the roots. As the germ is always growing warm, the moisture, pumped up through the roots, and helped by the attraction of heat, draws a proper amount of nourishment from the soil, and distributes it to the stem, to the bark, to the husk, to the seed itself and to the beards with which it is armed. It is owing to these successive accretions that each plant attains its natural development, as well corn as vegetables, herbs or brushwood. A single plant, a blade of grass is sufficient to occupy all your intelligence in the contemplation of the skill which produced it. [175] Why is the wheat stalk better with joints? [176] Are they not like fastenings, which help it to bear easily the weight of the ear, when it is swollen with fruit and bends towards the earth? Thus, whilst oats, which have no weight to bear at the top, are without these supports, nature has provided them for wheat. It has hidden the grain in a case, so that it may not be exposed to birds' pillage, and has furnished it

---

[175] "To me the meanest flower that blows can give Thoughts that do often lie too deep for tears." Wordsworth, Ode on Immortality.

[176] Literally, knee—Latin geniculum. cf. Xen., Anab. iv. 5, 26, and Theoph. viii. 2, 4. "Knee-jointed" is a recognised English term for certain grasses.

The Haxaemeron - St Basil

with a rampart of barbs, which, like darts, protect it against the attacks of tiny creatures.

4. What shall I say? What shall I leave unsaid? In the rich treasures of creation it is difficult to select what is most precious; the loss of what is omitted is too severe. "Let the earth bring forth grass;" and instantly, with useful plants, appear noxious plants; with corn, hemlock; with the other nutritious plants, hellebore, monkshood, mandrake and the juice of the poppy. What then? Shall we show no gratitude for so many beneficial gifts, and reproach the Creator for those which may be harmful to our life? And shall we not reflect that all has not been created in view of the wants of our bellies? The nourishing plants, which are destined for our use, are close at hand, and known by all the world. But in creation nothing exists without a reason. The blood of the bull is a poison:[177] ought this animal then, whose strength is so serviceable to man, not to have been created, or, if created, to have been bloodless? But you have sense enough in yourself to keep you free from deadly things. What! Sheep and goats know how to turn away from what threatens their life, discerning danger by instinct alone: and you, who have reason and the art of medicine to supply what you need, and the experience of your forebears to tell you to avoid all that is dangerous, you tell me that you find it difficult to keep yourself from poisons! But not a single thing has been created without reason, not a single thing is useless. One serves as food to some animal; medicine has found in another a relief for one of our maladies. Thus the starling eats

---

[177] "Taurorum (sanguis) pestifer potu maxime." Plin. xi. 90. Taurinus recens inter venena est. 2d. xxviii. 41. cf. Dioscorid. in Alexiph. 25.

hemlock, its constitution rendering it insusceptible to the action of the poison. Thanks to the tenuity of the pores of its heart, the malignant juice is no sooner swallowed than it is digested, before its chill can attack the vital parts.[178] The quail, thanks to its peculiar temperament, whereby it escapes the dangerous effects, feeds on hellebore. There are even circumstances where poisons are useful to men; with mandrake[179] doctors give us sleep; with opium they lull violent pain. Hemlock has ere now been used to appease the rage of unruly diseases;[180] and many times hellebore has taken away long standing disease.[181] These plants, then, instead of making you accuse the Creator, give you a new subject for gratitude.

5. "Let the earth bring forth grass." What spontaneous provision is included in these words,–that which is present in the root, in the plant itself, and in the fruit, as well as that which our labour and husbandry add! God did not command the earth immediately to give forth seed and fruit, but to produce germs, to grow green, and to arrive at maturity in the seed; so that this first command teaches nature what she has to do in the course of ages. But, they ask, is it true that the earth produces seed after his kind, when often, after having sown wheat, we gather black grain? This is not a change of kind, but an alteration, a disease of the

---

[178] cf. Galen. De Simp. Pac. iii.

[179] ho mandragoras tous anthropous koimizei. Xen., Symp. ii. 24.

[180] cf. Arataeus, De Morb. Aent. ii. 11.

[181] The Black Hellebore, or Christmas Rose, is a recognised alternative. Whether this is the plant of Anticyra is doubtful.

The Haxaemeron - St Basil

grain. It has not ceased to be wheat; it is on account of having been burnt that it is black, as one can learn from its name. [182] If a severe frost had burnt it, [183] it would have had another colour and a different flavour. They even pretend that, if it could find suitable earth and moderate temperature, it might return to its first form. Thus, you find nothing in nature contrary to the divine command. As to the darnel and all those bastard grains which mix themselves with the harvest, the tares of Scripture, far from being a variety of corn, have their own origin and their own kind; image of those who alter the doctrine of the Lord and, not being rightly instructed in the word, but, corrupted by the teaching of the evil one, mix themselves with the sound body of the Church to spread their pernicious errors secretly among purer souls. The Lord thus compares the perfection of those who believe in Him to the growth of seed, "as if a man should cast seed into the ground; and should sleep and rise, night and day, and the seed should spring and grow up, he knoweth not how. For the earth bringeth forth fruit of herself; first the blade, then the ear, after that the full corn in the ear."[184] "Let the earth bring forth grass." In a moment earth began by germination to obey the laws of the Creator, completed every stage of growth, and brought germs to perfection. The meadows were

---

[182] puros=wheat. The root, which has nothing to do with pur, is found by Curtius in the Slavonic pyro=rye, the Bohemian pyr=quitch grass, the Lettish purji=wheat, and the Lithuanian pyragas=wheaten bread. (L. & S. in loc.)

[183] cf. Virg., Georg. i. 93: "Aut Boreae penetrabile frigus adurat." Ov. M. xiv. 763, Frigus adurat poma, and in Greek Arist., Meteor. iv. 5.

[184] Matt. iv. 26-28.

The Haxaemeron - St Basil

covered with deep grass, the fertile plains quivered[185] with harvests, and the movement of the corn was like the waving of the sea. Every plant, every herb, the smallest shrub, the least vegetable, arose from the earth in all its luxuriance. There was no failure in this first vegetation: no husbandman's inexperience, no inclemency of the weather, nothing could injure it; then the sentence of condemnation was not fettering the earth's fertility. All this was before the sin which condemned us to eat our bread by the sweat of our brow.

6. "Let the earth," the Creator adds, "bring forth the fruit tree yielding fruit after his kind, whose seed is in itself."[186]

At this command every copse was thickly planted; all the trees, fir, cedar, cypress, pine, rose to their greatest height, the shrubs were straightway clothed with thick foliage.[187] The plants called crown-plants, roses, myrtles, laurels, did not exist; in one moment they came into being, each one with its distinctive peculiarities. Most marked differences separated them from other plants, and each one was distinguished by a character of its own. But then the rose was without thorns; since then the thorn has been added to its beauty, to make us feel that sorrow is very near to pleasure, and to remind us of our sin, which

---

[185] cf. Horrescunt segetes. Virg.,Georg. iii. 39.

[186] Gen. i. 11.

[187] amphikomoi kai daseis. cf. Milton, "With frizzled hair implicit." P.L. vii.

condemned the earth to produce thorns[188] and caltrops. But, they say, the earth has received the command to produce trees "yielding fruit whose seed was in itself," and we see many trees which have neither fruit, nor seed. What shall we reply? First, that only the more important trees are mentioned; and then, that a careful examination will show us that every tree has seed, or some property which takes the place of it. The black poplar, the willow, the elm, the white poplar, all the trees of this family, do not produce any apparent fruit; however, an attentive observer finds seed in each of them. This grain which is at the base of the leaf, and which those who busy themselves with inventing words call mischos, has the property of seed. And there are trees which reproduce by their branches, throwing out roots from them. Perhaps we ought even to consider as seeds the saplings which spring from the roots of a tree: for cultivators tear them out to multiply the species. But, we have already said, it is chiefly a question of the trees which contribute most to our life; which offer their various fruits to man and provide him with plentiful nourishment. Such is the vine, which produces wine to make glad the heart of man; such is the olive tree, whose fruit brightens his face with oil. How many things in nature are combined in the same plant! In a vine, roots, green and flexible branches, which spread themselves far over the earth, buds, tendrils, bunches of sour grapes and ripe grapes. The sight of a vine, when observed by an intelligent eye, serves to remind you of your nature. Without doubt you remember the parable where the Lord calls Himself a vine and His Father the husbandman, and

---

[188] cf. Milton, P.L., B. iv., "Flowers of all hue and without thorn the rose," and August. De Genesi contra Manichaeos. i. 13.

every one of us who are grafted by faith into the Church the branches. He invites us to produce fruits in abundance, for fear lest our sterility should condemn us to the fire.[189] He constantly compares our souls to vines. "My well beloved," says He, "hath a vineyard in a very fruitfull hill,"[190] and elsewhere, I have "planted a vineyard and hedged it round about."[191] Evidently He calls human souls His vine, those souls whom He has surrounded with the authority of His precepts and a guard of angels. "The angel of the Lord encampeth round about them that fear him."[192] And further: He has planted for us, so to say, props, in establishing in His Church apostles, prophets, teachers;[193] and raising our thoughts by the example of the blessed in olden times, He has not allowed them to drag on the earth and be crushed under foot. He wishes that the claspings of love, like the tendrils of the vine, should attach us to our neighbours and make us rest on them, so that, in our continual aspirations towards heaven, we may imitate these vines, which raise themselves to the tops of the tallest trees. He also asks us to allow ourselves to be dug about; and that is what the soul does when it disembarrasses itself from the cares of the world, which are a weight on our hearts. He, then, who is freed from carnal affections and from the love of riches, and, far from being dazzled by them, disdains

---

[189] cf. S. John xv. 1-6.

[190] Isa. v. 1.

[191] Matt. xxi. 33.

[192] Ps. xxxiv. 7.

[193] cf. 1 Cor. xii. 28.

and despises this miserable vain glory, is, so to say, dug about and at length breathes, free from the useless weight of earthly thoughts. Nor must we, in the spirit of the parable, put forth too much wood, that is to say, live with ostentation, and gain the applause of the world; we must bring forth fruits, keeping the proof of our works for the husbandman. Be "like a green olive tree in the house of God,"[194] never destitute of hope, but decked through faith with the bloom of salvation. Thus you will resemble the eternal verdure of this plant and will rival it in fruitfulness, if each day sees you giving abundantly in alms.

7. But let us return to the examination of the ingenious contrivances of creation. How many trees then arose, some to give us their fruits, others to roof our houses, others to build our ships, others to feed our fires! What a variety in the disposition of their several parts! And yet, how difficult is it to find the distinctive property of each of them, and to grasp the difference which separates them from other species. Some strike deep roots, others do not; some shoot straight up and have only one stem, others appear to love the earth and, from their root upwards, divide into several shoots. Those whose long branches stretch up afar into the air, have also deep roots which spread within a large circumference, a true foundation placed by nature to support the weight of the tree. What variety there is in bark! Some plants have smooth bark, others rough, some have only one layer, others several. What a marvellous thing! You may find in the youth and age of plants resemblances to those of man. Young and vigorous, their bark is distended;

---

[194] Ps. lii. 8.

when they grow old, it is rough and wrinkled. Cut one, it sends forth new buds; the other remains henceforward sterile and as if struck with a mortal wound. But further, it has been observed that pines, cut down, or even submitted to the action of fire, are changed into a forest of oaks.[195] We know besides that the industry of agriculturists remedies the natural defects of certain trees. Thus the sharp pomegranate and bitter almonds, if the trunk of the tree is pierced near the root to introduce into the middle of the pith a fat plug of pine, lose the acidity of their juice, and become delicious fruits.[196] Let not the sinner then despair of himself, when he thinks, if agriculture can change the juices of plants, the efforts of the soul to arrive at virtue, can certainly triumph over all infirmities.

---

[195] The phenomenon has been observed in later days, though Basil may be at fault in his account of the cause. When pines have been cleared away in North American forests young oaklings have sprung up. The acorn lay long hid, unable to contend against the pine, but, when once the ground was clear, it sprouted. This upgrowth of a new kind of tree had been accounted for partly by the burial of germs by jays, rooks, and some quadrupeds; partly by the theory of De Candolle and Liebig that roots expel certain substances which, though unfavourable to the vitality of the plant excreting them, are capable of supporting others. So, on the pine pressure being removed, the hidden seeds sprout in a kind of vegetable manure. cf. Sir Charles Lvell's Travels in the United States and Rough's Elements of Forestry, p. 19.

[196] Ambrose, Hexaem. iii. 13, writes: Amygdalis quoque hoc genere medicari feruntur agricolae, ut ex amaris dulces fiant fructus, ut et terebrent ejus radicem arboris, et in medium inserant surculum ejus arboris quam Graeci peuchen, nos piceam dicimus: quo facto succi amaritudo deponitur.

Now there is such a variety of fruits in fruit trees that it is beyond all expression; a variety not only in the fruits of trees of different families, but even in those of the same species, if it be true, as gardeners say, that the sex of a tree influences the character of its fruits. They distinguish male from female in palms; sometimes we see those which they call female lower their branches, as though with passionate desire, and invite the embraces of the male. Then, those who take care of these plants shake over these palms the fertilizing dust from the male palm-tree, the psen as they call it: the tree appears to share the pleasures of enjoyment; then it raises its branches, and its foliage resumes its usual form. The same is said of the fig tree. Some plant wild fig trees near cultivated fig trees, and there are others who, to remedy the weakness of the productive fig tree of our gardens, attach to the branches unripe figs and so retain the fruit which had already begun to drop and to be lost. What lesson does nature here give us? That we must often borrow, even from those who are strangers to the faith, a certain vigour to show forth good works. If you see outside the Church, in pagan life, or in the midst of a pernicious heresy, the example of virtue and fidelity to moral laws, redouble your efforts to resemble the productive fig tree, who by the side of the wild fig tree, gains strength, prevents the fruit from being shed, and nourishes it with more care.

8. Plants reproduce themselves in so many different ways, that we can only touch upon the chief among them. As to fruits themselves, who could review their varieties, their forms, their colours, the peculiar flavour, and the use of each of them? Why do some fruits ripen when exposed bare to the rays of the sun,

while others fill out while encased in shells? Trees of which the fruit is tender have, like the fig tree, a thick shade of leaves; those, on the contrary, of which the fruits are stouter, like the nut, are only covered by a light shade. The delicacy of the first requires more care; if the latter had a thicker case, the shade of the leaves would be harmful. Why is the vine leaf serrated, if not that the bunches of grapes may at the same time resist the injuries of the air and receive through the openings all the rays of the sun? Nothing has been done without motive, nothing by chance. All shows ineffable wisdom.[197]

What discourse can touch all? Can the human mind make an exact review, remark every distinctive property, exhibit all the differences, unveil with certainty so many mysterious causes? The same water, pumped up through the root, nourishes in a different way the root itself, the bark of the trunk, the wood and the pith. It becomes leaf, it distributes itself among the branches and twigs and makes the fruits swell–it gives to the plant its gum and its sap. Who will explain to us the difference between all these? There is a difference between the gum of the mastich

---

[197] On the argument from design, cf. Aristotle, De Part. Anim. iii. 1, as quoted and translated by Cudworth, III. xxxvii. 3: "A carpenter would give a better account than so, for he would not think it sufficient to say that the fabric came to be of such a form because the instruments happened to fall so and so, but he will tell you that it is because himself made such strokes, and that he directed the instruments and determined their motion after such a manner, to this end that he might make the whole a fabric fit and useful for such purposes." On the strength and weakness of the argument from design, in view of modern speculation, suggestive matter is contained in Dr. Eagar's Buther's Analogy and Modern Thought, p. 49 et sq.

and the juice of the balsam, a difference between that which distils in Egypt and Libya from the fennel. Amber is, they say, the crystallized sap of plants. And for a proof, see the bits of straws and little insects which have been caught in the sap while still liquid and imprisoned there. In one word, no one without long experience could find terms to express the virtue of it. How, again, does this water become wine in the vine, and oil in the olive tree? Yet what is marvellous is, not to see it become sweet in one fruit, fat and unctuous in another, but to see in sweet fruits an inexpressible variety of flavour. There is one sweetness of the grape, another of the apple, another of the fig, another of the date. I shall willingly give you the gratification of continuing this research. How is it that this same water has sometimes a sweet taste, softened by its remaining in certain plants, and at other times stings the palate because it has become acid by passing through others? How is it, again, that it attains extreme bitterness, and makes the mouth rough when it is found in wormwood and in scammony? That it has in acorns and dogwood a sharp and rough flavour? That in the turpentine tree and the walnut tree it is changed into a soft and oily matter?

9. But what need is there to continue, when in the same fig tree we have the most opposite flavours, as bitter in the sap as it is sweet in the fruit? And in the vine, is it not as sweet in the grapes as it is astringent in the branches? And what a variety of colour! Look how in a meadow this same water becomes red in one flower, purple in another, blue in this one, white in that. And this diversity of colours, is it to be compared to that of scents? But I perceive that an insatiable

curiosity is drawing out my discourse beyond its limits. If I do not stop and recall it to the law of creation, day will fail me whilst making you see great wisdom in small things.

"Let the earth bring forth the fruit tree yielding fruit." Immediately the tops of the mountains were covered with foliage: paradises were artfully laid out, and an infinitude of plants embellished the banks of the rivers. Some were for the adornment of man's table; some to nourish animals with their fruits and their leaves; some to provide medicinal help by giving us their sap, their juice, their chips, their bark or their fruit. In a word, the experience of ages, profiting from every chance, has not been able to discover anything useful, which the penetrating foresight of the Creator did not first perceive and call into existence. Therefore, when you see the trees in our gardens, or those of the forest, those which love the water or the land, those which bear flowers, or those which do not flower, I should like to see you recognising grandeur even in small objects, adding incessantly to your admiration of, and redoubling your love for the Creator. Ask yourself why He has made some trees evergreen and others deciduous; why, among the first, some lose their leaves, and others always keep them. Thus the olive and the pine shed their leaves, although they renew them insensibly and never appear to be despoiled of their verdure. The palm tree, on the contrary, from its birth to its death, is always adorned with the same foliage. Think again of the double life of the tamarisk; it is an aquatic plant, and yet it covers the desert. Thus, Jeremiah

The Haxaemeron - St Basil

compares it to the worst of characters—the double character.[198]

10. "Let the earth bring forth." This short command was in a moment a vast nature, an elaborate system. Swifter than thought it produced the countless qualities of plants. It is this command which, still at this day, is imposed on the earth, and in the course of each year displays all the strength of its power to produce herbs, seeds and trees. Like tops, which after the first impulse, continue their evolutions, turning upon themselves when once fixed in their centre; thus nature, receiving the impulse of this first command, follows without interruption the course of ages, until the consummation of all things.[199] Let us all hasten to attain to it, full of fruit and of good works; and thus, planted in the house of the Lord we shall flourish in the court of our God, [200] in our Lord Jesus

---

[198] cf. Jer. xvii. 6, LXX.

[199] "Ac mihi quidem videtur, cum duae sententiae fuissent veterum philosophorum, una eorum qui censerent omnia ita fato fieri, ut id fatum vim necessitatis afferret, in qua sententia Democritus, Heraclitus, Empedocles, Aristoteles fuit; altera eorum, quibus viderentur sine ullo fato esse animorum motus voluntarii: Chrysippus tanquam arbiter honorarius, medium ferire voluisse...quanquam assensio non possit fieri nisi commota visa, tamen cum id visum proximam causam habeat, non principalem hanc habet rationem, ut Chrysippus vult, quam dudum diximus, non, ut illa quidem fieri possit, nulla vi extrinsecus excitata, necesse est enim assensionem viso commoveri, sed revertitur ad cylindrum, et ad turbinem suum, quae moveri incipere, nisi pulsa non possunt: id autem cum accidit suapte natura, quod superest et cylindrum volvi, et versari turbinem putat." (Cic., De fato. xviii.)

[200] cf. Ps. xcii. 13.

Christ, to whom be glory and power for ever and ever. Amen.

Homily VI

The creation of luminous bodies.

1. At the shows in the circus the spectator must join in the efforts of the athletes. This the laws of the show indicate, for they prescribe that all should have the head uncovered when present at the stadium. The object of this, in my opinion, is that each one there should not only be a spectator of the athletes, but be, in a certain measure, a true athlete himself.[201] Thus, to investigate the great and prodigious show of creation, to understand supreme and ineffable wisdom, you must bring personal light for the contemplation of the wonders which I spread before your eyes, and help me, according to your power, in this struggle, where you are not so much judges as fellow combatants,[202] for fear lest the truth might escape you, and lest my error might turn to your common prejudice. Why these words? It is because we propose to study the world as a whole, and to consider the universe, not by the light of worldly wisdom, but by that with which God wills to enlighten His servant, when He speaks to him in person and without enigmas. It is because it is absolutely necessary that all lovers of great and grand shows should bring a mind well prepared to study

---

[201] In the Theatrum spectators might be covered. cf. Mart. xiv. 29: "In Pompeiano tectus spectabo theatro; Nam ventus populo vela negare solet." cf. Dion Cassius lix. 7. These passages may, however, indicate exceptional cases.

[202] cf. Greg., In Ez.: Propter bonos auditores malis doctoribus sermo datur: et propter malos auditores bonis doctoribus sermo subtrahitur.

The Haxaemeron - St Basil

them. If sometimes, on a bright night,[203] whilst gazing with watchful eyes on the inexpressible beauty of the stars, you have thought of the Creator of all things; if you have asked yourself who it is that has dotted heaven with such flowers, and why visible things are even more useful than beautiful; if sometimes, in the day, you have studied the marvels of light, if you have raised yourself by visible things to the invisible Being, then you are a well prepared auditor, and you can take your place in this august and blessed amphitheatre. Come in the same way that any one not knowing a town is taken by the hand and led through it; thus I am going to lead you, like strangers, through the mysterious marvels of this great city of the universe.[204] Our first country was in this great city, whence the murderous daemon whose enticements seduced man to slavery expelled us. There you will see man's first origin and his immediate seizure by death, brought forth by sin, the first born of the evil spirit. You will know that you are formed of earth, but

---

[203] "By night an atheist half believes in God." Young, N.T. v. 177. cf. also Cic., De nat. Deor. ii. 38: Quis enim hunc hominem dixerit, qui tam certos coeli motus, tam ratos astrorum ordines, tamque omnia ister se connexa et apta viderit, neget in his ullam inesse rationem, eaque casu fieri dicat, quae quanto consilio gerantur, nullo consilio assequi possumus.

[204] cf. Cic., De Nat. Deor. ii. 62. Est enim mundus quasi communis deorum atque hominum domus, aut urbs utrorumque. Soli etiam ratione utentes, jure ac lege vivunt. Bp. Lightfoot quotes in illustration of Phil. iii. 20, Philo, De Conf. i. 416, M. patrida men ton ouranion choron en ho politeuontai xenon de ton perigeion en ho parokesan nomizousai. So Clem. Alex., Strom. iv. 26, legousi gar hoi Stoikoi ton men ouranon kurios polin ta de epi ges entautha ouk eti poleis, legesthai gar, ouk einai de, and Plato, Rep. ix. 592, B. en ourano isos paradeigma (tes poleos) anakeitai to boulomeno horan kai horonti heauton katoikizein.

the work of God's hands; much weaker than the brute, but ordained to command beings without reason and soul; inferior as regards natural advantages, but, thanks to the privilege of reason, capable of raising yourself to heaven. If we are penetrated by these truths, we shall know ourselves, we shall know God, we shall adore our Creator, we shall serve our Master, we shall glorify our Father, we shall love our Sustainer, we shall bless our Benefactor, we shall not cease to honour the Prince [205] of present and future life, Who, by the riches that He showers upon us in this world, makes us believe in His promises and uses present good things to strengthen our expectation of the future. Truly, if such are the good things of time, what will be those of eternity? If such is the beauty of visible things, what shall we think of invisible things? If the grandeur of heaven exceeds the measure of human intelligence, what mind shall be able to trace the nature of the everlasting? If the sun, subject to corruption, is so beautiful, so grand, so rapid in its movement, so invariable in its course; if its grandeur is in such perfect harmony with and due proportion to the universe: if, by the beauty of its nature, it shines like a brilliant eye in the middle of creation; if finally, one cannot tire of contemplating it, what will be the beauty of the Sun of Righteousness? [206] If the blind man suffers from not seeing the material sun, what a deprivation is it for the sinner not to enjoy the true light!

2. "And God said, Let there be lights in the firmament of the heaven to give light upon the earth, and to

---

[205] cf. Acts iii. 15.

[206] cf. Mal. iv. 2.

divide the day from the night."[207] Heaven and earth were the first; after them was created light; the day had been distinguished from the night, then had appeared the firmament and the dry element. The water had been gathered into the reservoir assigned to it, the earth displayed its productions, it had caused many kinds of herbs to germinate and it was adorned with all kinds of plants. However, the sun and the moon did not yet exist, in order that those who live in ignorance of God may not consider the sun as the origin and the father of light, or as the maker of all that grows out of the earth.[208] That is why there was a fourth day, and then God said: "Let there be lights in the firmament of the heaven."

When once you have learnt Who spoke, think immediately of the hearer. God said, "Let there be lights…and God made two great lights." Who spoke? and Who made? Do you not see a double person? Everywhere, in mystic language, history is sown with the dogmas of theology.

---

[207] Gen. i. 14, LXX.

[208] Fialon quotes Bossuet (5th elev. 3d week): "Ainsi il a fait la lumiere avant que de faire les grands luminaires ou il a voulu la ramasser: et il a fait la distinction des jours avant que d'avoir cree les astres dont il s'est servi pour les regler parfaitement: et le soir et le matin ont ete distingues, avant que leur distinction et la division parfaite du jour et de la nuit fut bien marquee; et les arbres, et les arbustes, et les herbes ont germe sur la terre par ordre de Dieu, avant qu'il eut fait le soleil, qui devait etre le pere de toutes ces plantes; et il a detache expres les effets d'avec leurs causes naturelles, pour montrer que naturellement tout ne tient qu'`a lui seul, et ne depend que de sa seule volonte."

The Haxaemeron - St Basil

The motive follows which caused the lights to be created. It was to illuminate the earth. Already light was created; why therefore say that the sun was created to give light? And, first, do not laugh at the strangeness of this expression. We do not follow your nicety about words, and we trouble ourselves but little to give them a harmonious turn. Our writers do not amuse themselves by polishing their periods, and everywhere we prefer clearness of words to sonorous expressions. See then if by this expression "to light up," the sacred writer sufficiently made his thought understood. He has put "to give light"[209] instead of "illumination."[210] Now there is nothing here contradictory to what has been said of light. Then the actual nature of light was produced: now the sun's body is constructed to be a vehicle for that original light. A lamp is not fire. Fire has the property of illuminating, and we have invented the lamp to light us in darkness. In the same way, the luminous bodies have been fashioned as a vehicle for that pure, clear, and immaterial light. The Apostle speaks to us of certain lights which shine in the world[211] without being confounded with the true light of the world, the possession of which made the saints luminaries of the souls which they instructed and drew from the darkness of ignorance. This is why the Creator of all things, made the sun in addition to that glorious light, and placed it shining in the heavens.

---

[209] phausis, the act of giving light, LXX.

[210] photismos, the condition produced by phausis.

[211] cf. Phil. ii. 15.

The Haxaemeron - St Basil

3. And let no one suppose it to be a thing incredible that the brightness of the light is one thing, and the body which is its material vehicle is another. First, in all composite things, we distinguish substance susceptible of quality, and the quality which it receives. The nature of whiteness is one thing, another is that of the body which is whitened; thus the natures differ which we have just seen reunited by the power of the Creator. And do not tell me that it is impossible to separate them. Even I do not pretend to be able to separate light from the body of the sun; but I maintain that that which we separate in thought, may be separated in reality by the Creator of nature. You cannot, moreover, separate the brightness of fire from the virtue of burning which it possesses; but God, who wished to attract His servant by a wonderful sight, set a fire in the burning bush, which displayed all the brilliancy of flame while its devouring property was dormant. It is that which the Psalmist affirms in saying "The voice of the Lord divideth the flames of fire."[212] Thus, in the requital which awaits us after this life, a mysterious voice seems to tell us that the double nature of fire will be divided; the just will enjoy its light, and the torment of its heat will be the torture of the wicked.

In the revolutions of the moon we find anew proof of what we have advanced. When it stops and grows less it does not consume itself in all its body, but in the measure that it deposits or absorbs the light which surrounds it, it presents to us the image of its decrease or of its increase. If we wish an evident proof that the moon does not consume its body when

---

[212] Ps. xxix. 7.

at rest, we have only to open our eyes. If you look at it in a cloudless and clear sky, you observe, when it has taken the complete form of a crescent, that the part, which is dark and not lighted up, describes a circle equal to that which the full moon forms. Thus the eye can take in the whole circle, if it adds to the illuminated part this obscure and dark curve. And do not tell me that the light of the moon is borrowed, diminishing or increasing in proportion as it approaches or recedes from the sun. That is not now the object of our research; we only wish to prove that its body differs from the light which makes it shine. I wish you to have the same idea of the sun; except however that the one, after having once received light and having mixed it with its substance, does not lay it down again, whilst the other, turn by turn, putting off and reclothing itself again with light, proves by that which takes place in itself what we have said of the sun.

The sun and moon thus received the command to divide the day from the night. God had already separated light from darkness; then He placed their natures in opposition, so that they could not mingle, and that there could never be anything in common between darkness and light. You see what a shadow is during the day; that is precisely the nature of darkness during the night. If, at the appearance of a light, the shadow always falls on the opposite side; if in the morning it extends towards the setting sun; if in the evening it inclines towards the rising sun, and at mid-day turns towards the north; night retires into the regions opposed to the rays of the sun, since it is by nature only the shadow of the earth. Because, in the same way that, during the day, shadow is produced by a body which intercepts the light, night comes naturally when the air which surrounds the earth is in shadow. And this is precisely what Scripture says, "God divided the light from the darkness." Thus darkness fled at the approach of light, the two being at their first creation divided by a natural antipathy. Now God commanded the sun to measure the day, and the moon, whenever she rounds her disc, to rule the night. For then these two luminaries are almost diametrically opposed; when the sun rises, the full moon disappears from the horizon, to re-appear in the east at the moment the sun sets. It matters little to our subject if in other phases the light of the moon does not correspond exactly with night. It is none the less true, that when at its perfection it makes the stars to turn pale and lightens up the earth with the splendour of its light, it reigns over the night, and in concert with the sun divides the duration of it in equal parts.

4. "And let them be for signs, and for seasons, and for days and years."[213] The signs which the luminaries give are necessary to human life. In fact what useful observations will long experience make us discover, if we ask without undue curiosity! What signs of rain, of drought, or of the rising of the wind, partial or general, violent or moderate! Our Lord indicates to us one of the signs given by the sun when He says, "It will be foul weather to-day; for the sky is red and lowering."[214] In fact, when the sun rises through a fog, its rays are darkened, but the disc appears burning like a coal and of a bloody red colour. It is the thickness of the air which causes this appearance; as

---

[213] Gen. i. 14.

[214] St. Matt. xvi. 3.

The Haxaemeron - St Basil

the rays of the sun do not disperse such amassed and condensed air, it cannot certainly be retained by the waves of vapour which exhale from the earth, and it will cause from superabundance of moisture a storm in the countries over which it accumulates. In the same way, when the moon is surrounded with moisture, or when the sun is encircled with what is called a halo, it is the sign of heavy rain or of a violent storm; again, in the same way, if mock suns accompany the sun in its course they foretell certain celestial phenomena. Finally, those straight lines, like the colours of the rainbow, which are seen on the clouds, announce rain, extraordinary tempests, or, in one word, a complete change in the weather.

Those who devote themselves to the observation of these bodies find signs in the different phases of the moon, as if the air, by which the earth is enveloped, were obliged to vary to correspond with its change of form. Towards the third day of the new moon, if it is sharp and clear, it is a sign of fixed fine weather. If its horns appear thick and reddish it threatens us either with heavy rain or with a gale from the South.[215] Who does not know how useful [216] are these signs in life? Thanks to them, the sailor keeps back his vessel in the harbour, foreseeing the perils with which the winds threaten him, and the traveller beforehand takes shelter from harm, waiting until the weather has

---

[215] pante gar kathare ke mal' eudia tekmeraio, panta d' ereuthomene dokeein anemoio keleuthous, allothi d' allo melainomene dokeein huetoio. Aratus 70.

[216] cf. Verg., Georg. i. 424: Si vero solem ad rapidum lunasque sequentes Ordine respicies, nunquam te crastina fallet Hora, neque insidiis noctis capiere serenae.

The Haxaemeron - St Basil

become fairer. Thanks to them, husbandmen, busy with sowing seed or cultivating plants, are able to know which seasons are favourable to their labours. Further, the Lord has announced to us that at the dissolution of the universe, signs will appear in the sun, in the moon and in the stars. The sun shall be turned into blood and the moon shall not give her light, [217] signs of the consummation of all things.

5. But those who overstep the borders,[218] making the words of Scripture their apology for the art of casting nativities, pretend that our lives depend upon the motion of the heavenly bodies, and that thus the Chaldaeans read in the planets that which will happen to us. [219] By these very simple words "let them be for signs," they understand neither the variations of the

---

[217] Basil seems to be confusing Joel ii. 31 and Matt. xxiv. 29.

[218] huper ta eskammena pedan is a proverbial phrase for going beyond bounds. cf. Lucian., Gall. vi. and Plat., Crat. 413, a.

[219] "On doit d'autant plus louer le grand sens de Saint Basile qui s'inspire presqu' entierement d'Origene et de Plotin, sans tomber dans leur erreur. En riant toute espece de relation entre les astres et les actes de l'homme, il conserve intacte notre liberte." Fialon, p. 425. "Quale deinde judicium de hominum factis Deo relinquitur, quibus coelestis necessitas adhibetur cum Dominus ille sit et siderum et hominum. Aut si non dicunt stellas accepta quidam potestate a summo Deo, arbitrio suo ista decernere, sed in talibus necessitatibus ingerendis illius omnino jussa complere, ita ne de ipso Deo sentiendum est, quod indignissimum visum est de stellarum voluntate sentire. Quod si dicuntur stellae significare potius ista quam facere, ut quasi locutio sit quaedam illa positio praedicens futura, non agens (non enim mediocriter doctorum hominum fuit ista sententia) non quidem ita solent loqui mathematici, ut verbi gratia dicunt, Mars ita positus homicidam significat, sed homicidam non facit." August., De C. Dei. v. 1.

weather, nor the change of seasons; they only see in them, at the will of their imagination, the distribution of human destinies. What do they say in reality? When the planets cross in the signs of the Zodiac, certain figures formed by their meeting give birth to certain destinies, and others produce different destinies.

Perhaps for clearness sake it is not useless to enter into more detail about this vain science. I will say nothing of my own to refute them; I will use their words, bringing a remedy for the infected, and for others a preservative from falling. The inventors of astrology seeing that in the extent of time many signs escaped them, divided it and enclosed each part in narrow limits, as if in the least and shortest interval, in a moment, in the twinkling of an eye,[220] to speak with the Apostle, the greatest difference should be found between one birth and another. Such an one is born in this moment; he will be a prince over cities and will govern the people, in the fulness of riches and power. Another is born the instant after; he will be poor, miserable, and will wander daily from door to door begging his bread. Consequently they divide the Zodiac into twelve parts, and, as the sun takes thirty days to traverse each of the twelve divisions of this unerring circle, they divide them into thirty more. Each of them forms sixty new ones, and these last are again divided into sixty. Let us see then if, in determining the birth of an infant, it will be possible to observe this rigorous division of time. The child is born. The nurse ascertains the sex; then she awaits the wail which is a sign of its life. Until then how many moments have passed do you think? The nurse

---

[220] 1 Cor. xv. 52.

announces the birth of the child to the Chaldaean: how many minutes would you count before she opens her mouth, especially if he who records the hour is outside the women's apartments? And we know that he who consults the dial, ought, whether by day or by night, to mark the hour with the most precise exactitude. What a swarm of seconds passes during this time! For the planet of nativity ought to be found, not only in one of the twelve divisions of the Zodiac, and even in one of its first subdivisions, but again in one of the sixtieth parts which divide this last, and even, to arrive at the exact truth, in one of the sixtieth subdivisions that this contains in its turn. And to obtain such minute knowledge, so impossible to grasp from this moment, each planet must be questioned to find its position as regards the signs of the Zodiac and the figures that the planets form at the moment of the child's birth. Thus, if it is impossible to find exactly the hour of birth, and if the least change can upset all, then both those who give themselves up to this imaginary science and those who listen to them open-mouthed, as if they could learn from them the future, are supremely ridiculous.

6. But what effects are produced? Such an one will have curly hair and bright eyes, because he is born under the Ram; such is the appearance of a ram. He will have noble feelings; because the Ram is born to command. He will be liberal and fertile in resources, because this animal gets rid of its fleece without trouble, and nature immediately hastens to reclothe it. Another is born under the Bull: he will be enured to hardship and of a slavish character, because the bull bows under the yoke. Another is born under the Scorpion; like to this venomous reptile he will be a

The Haxaemeron - St Basil

striker. He who is born under the Balance will be just, thanks to the justness of our balances. Is not this the height of folly? This Ram, from whence you draw the nativity of man, is the twelfth part of the heaven, and in entering into it the sun reaches the spring. The Balance and the Bull are likewise twelfth parts of the Zodiac. How can you see there the principal causes which influence the life of man? And why do you take animals to characterize the manners of men who enter this world? He who is born under the Ram will be liberal, not because this part of heaven gives this characteristic, but because such is the nature of the beast. Why then should we frighten ourselves by the names of these stars and undertake to persuade ourselves with these bleatings? If heaven has different characteristics derived from these animals, it is then itself subject to external influences since its causes depend on the brutes who graze in our fields. A ridiculous assertion; but how much more ridiculous the pretence of arriving at the influence on each other of things which have not the least connexion! This pretended science is a true spider's web; if a gnat or a fly, or some insect equally feeble falls into it it is held entangled; if a stronger animal approaches, it passes through without trouble, carrying the weak tissue away with it. [221]

7. They do not, however, stop here; even our acts, where each one feels his will ruling, I mean, the practice of virtue or of vice, depend, according to them, on the influence of celestial bodies. It would be

---

[221] Elege de...tous nomous tois arachniois homoious; kai gar ekeina e& 129;n men empese ti kouphon kai asthenes stegein, e& 129;n de meizon, diakopsan oichesthai. Solon, in Diog. Laert. ii. 1.

The Haxaemeron - St Basil

ridiculous seriously to refute such an error, but, as it holds a great many in its nets, perhaps it is better not to pass it over in silence. I would first ask them if the figures which the stars describe do not change a thousand times a day. In the perpetual motion of planets, some meet in a more rapid course, others make slower revolutions, and often in an hour we see them look at each other and then hide themselves. Now, at the hour of birth, it is very important whether one is looked upon by a beneficent star or by an evil one, to speak their language. Often then the astrologers do not seize the moment when a good star shows itself, and, on account of having let this fugitive moment escape, they enrol the newborn under the influence of a bad genius. I am compelled to use their own words. What madness! But, above all, what impiety! For the evil stars throw the blame of their wickedness upon Him Who made them. If evil is inherent in their nature, the Creator is the author of evil. If they make it themselves, they are animals endowed with the power of choice, whose acts will be free and voluntary. Is it not the height of folly to tell these lies about beings without souls? Again, what a want of sense does it show to distribute good and evil without regard to personal merit; to say that a star is beneficent because it occupies a certain place; that it becomes evil, because it is viewed by another star; and that if it moves ever so little from this figure it loses its malign influence.

But let us pass on. If, at every instant of duration, the stars vary their figures, then in these thousand changes, many times a day, there ought to be reproduced the configuration of royal births. Why then does not every day see the birth of a king? Why is there a succession on the throne from father to son? Without doubt there has never been a king who has taken measures to have his son born under the star of royalty. For what man possesses such a power? How then did Uzziah beget Jotham, Jotham Ahaz, Ahaz Hezekiah? And by what chance did the birth of none of them happen in an hour of slavery? If the origin of our virtues and of our vices is not in ourselves, but is the fatal consequence of our birth, it is useless for legislators to prescribe for us what we ought to do, and what we ought to avoid; it is useless for judges to honour virtue and to punish vice. The guilt is not in the robber, not in the assassin: it was willed for him; it was impossible for him to hold back his hand, urged to evil by inevitable necessity. Those who laboriously cultivate the arts are the maddest of men. The labourer will make an abundant harvest without sowing seed and without sharpening his sickle. Whether he wishes it or not, the merchant will make his fortune, and will be flooded with riches by fate. As for us Christians, we shall see our great hopes vanish, since from the moment that man does not act with freedom, there is neither reward for justice, nor punishment for sin. Under the reign of necessity and of fatality there is no place for merit, the first condition of all righteous judgment. But let us stop. You who are sound in yourselves have no need to hear more, and time does not allow us to make attacks without limit against these unhappy men.

8. Let us return to the words which follow. "Let them be for signs and for seasons and for days and years." [222] We have spoken about signs. By times, we

---

[222] Gen. i. 14.

The Haxaemeron - St Basil

understand the succession of seasons, winter, spring, summer and autumn, which we see follow each other in so regular a course, thanks to the regularity of the movement of the luminaries. It is winter when the sun sojourns in the south and produces in abundance the shades of night in our region. The air spread over the earth is chilly, and the damp exhalations, which gather over our heads, give rise to rains, to frosts, to innumerable flakes of snow. When, returning from the southern regions, the sun is in the middle of the heavens and divides day and night into equal parts, the more it sojourns above the earth the more it brings back a mild temperature to us. Then comes spring, which makes all the plants germinate, and gives to the greater part of the trees their new life, and, by successive generation, perpetuates all the land and water animals. From thence the sun, returning to the summer solstice, in the direction of the North, gives us the longest days. And, as it travels farther in the air, it burns that which is over our heads, dries up the earth, ripens the grains and hastens the maturity of the fruits of the trees. At the epoch of its greatest heat, the shadows which the sun makes at mid-day are short, because it shines from above, from the air over our heads. Thus the longest days are those when the shadows are shortest, in the same way that the shortest days are those when the shadows are longest. It is this which happens to all of us "Hetero-skii"[223] (shadowed-on-one-side) who

---

[223] i.e. throwing a shadow only one way at noon,—said of those who live north and south of the tropics, while those who live in the tropics cast a shadow sometimes north, sometimes south, vide Strabo ii. 5. S: 43. It was "incredible" to Herodotus that Necho's Phoenician mariners, in their circumnavigation of Africa, had "the sun on their right hand." Her. iv. 42.

The Haxaemeron - St Basil

inhabit the northern regions of the earth. But there are people who, two days in the year, are completely without shade at mid-day, because the sun, being perpendicularly over their heads, lights them so equally from all sides, that it could through a narrow opening shine at the bottom of a well. Thus there are some who call them "askii" (shadowless). For those who live beyond the land of spices[224] see their shadow now on one side, now on another, the only inhabitants of this land of which the shade falls at mid-day; thus they are given the name of "amphiskii,"[225] (shadowed-on-both-sides). All these phenomena happen whilst the sun is passing into northern regions: they give us an idea of the heat thrown on the air, by the rays of the sun and of the effects that they produce. Next we pass to autumn, which breaks up the excessive heat, lessening the warmth little by little, and by a moderate temperature brings us back without suffering to winter, to the time when the sun returns from the northern regions to the southern. It is thus that seasons, following the course of the sun, succeed each other to rule our life.

"Let them be for days"[226] says Scripture, not to produce them but to rule them; because day and night are older than the creation of the luminaries and it is

---

[224] i.e. Arabia. cf. Lucan., Phars. iii. 247: Ignotum vobis Arabes venistis in orbem, Umbras mirati nemorum non ire sinistras.

[225] "Simili modo tradunt in Syene oppido, quod est super Alexandriam quinque millibus stadiorum, solstitii die medio nullam umbram jaci; puteumque ejus experimenti gratia factum, totum illuminari." Pliny ii. 75. cf. Lucan., Phars. 507, "atque umbras nunquam flectente Syene."

[226] Gen. i. 14.

this that the psalm declares to us. "The sun to rule by day...the moon and stars to rule by night."[227] How does the sun rule by day? Because carrying everywhere light with it, it is no sooner risen above the horizon than it drives away darkness and brings us day. Thus we might, without self deception, define day as air lighted by the sun, or as the space of time that the sun passes in our hemisphere. The functions of the sun and moon serve further to mark years. The moon, after having twelve times run her course, forms a year which sometimes needs an intercalary month to make it exactly agree with the seasons. Such was formerly the year of the Hebrews and of the early Greeks.[228] As to the solar year, it is the time that the sun, having started from a certain sign, takes to return to it in its normal progress.

9. "And God made two great lights."[229] The word "great," if, for example we say it of the heaven of the earth or of the sea, may have an absolute sense; but ordinarily it has only a relative meaning, as a great horse, or a great ox. It is not that these animals are of an immoderate size, but that in comparison with their like they deserve the title of great. What idea shall we ourselves form here of greatness? Shall it be the idea that we have of it in the ant and in all the little creatures of nature, which we call great in comparison

---

[227] Ps. cxxxvi. 8, 9.

[228] The Syrians and Macedonians had also an intercalary thirteenth month to accommodate the lunar to the solar cycle. Solon is credited with the introduction of the system into Greece about 594 b.c. But the Julian calendar improved upon this mode of adjustment.

[229] Gen. i. 16.

The Haxaemeron - St Basil

with those like themselves, and to show their superiority over them? Or shall we predicate greatness of the luminaries, as of the natural greatness inherent in them? As for me, I think so. If the sun and moon are great, it is not in comparison with the smaller stars, but because they have such a circumference that the splendour which they diffuse lights up the heavens and the air, embracing at the same time earth and sea. In whatever part of heaven they may be, whether rising, or setting, or in mid heaven, they appear always the same in the eyes of men, a manifest proof of their prodigious size. For the whole extent of heaven cannot make them appear greater in one place and smaller in another. Objects which we see afar off appear dwarfed to our eyes, and in measure as they approach us we can form a juster idea of their size. But there is no one who can be nearer or more distant from the sun. All the inhabitants of the earth see it at the same distance. Indians and Britons see it of the same size. The people of the East do not see it decrease in magnitude when it sets; those of the West do not find it smaller when it rises. If it is in the middle of the heavens it does not vary in either aspect. Do not be deceived by mere appearance, and because it looks a cubit's breadth, imagine it to be no bigger. [230] At a very great distance objects always lose size in our

---

[230] "Tertia ex utroque vastitas solis aperitur, ut non sit necesse amplitudinem ejus oculorum argumentis, atque conjectura animi scrutari: immensum esse quia arborum in limitibus porrectarum in quotlibet passuum millia umbras paribus jaciat intervallis, tanquam toto spatio medius: et quia per aequinoctium omnibus in meridiana plaga habitantibus, simul fiat a vertice: ita quia circa solstitialem circulum habitantium meridie ad Septemtrionem umbrae cadant, ortu vero ad occasum. Quae fieri nullo modo possent nisi multo quam terra major esset." Plin. ii. 8.

eyes; sight, not being able to clear the intermediary space, is as it were exhausted in the middle of its course, and only a small part of it reaches the visible object.[231] Our power of sight is small and makes all we see seem small, affecting what it sees by its own condition. Thus, then, if sight is mistaken its testimony is fallible. Recall your own impressions and you will find in yourself the proof of my words. If you have ever from the top of a high mountain looked at a large and level plain, how big did the yokes of oxen appear to you? How big were the ploughmen themselves? Did they not look like ants?[232] If from the top of a commanding rock, looking over the wide sea, you cast your eyes over the vast extent how big did the greatest islands appear to you? How large did one of those barks of great tonnage, which unfurl their white sails to the blue sea, appear to you. Did it not look smaller than a dove? It is because sight, as I have just told you, loses itself in the air, becomes weak and cannot seize with exactness the object which it sees. And further: your sight shows you high mountains

---

[231] Platon kata sunaugeian, tou men ek ton ophthalmon photos epi poson apor& 191;eontos eis ton homogene a& 153;ra, tou de apo tou somatos pheromenou apor& 191;ein; ton de metaxu a& 153;ra eudiachuton onta kai eutrepton, sunekteinontos to purodei tes opseos, haute, legetai platonike sunaugeia. Plut. peri ton aresk. iv. 13. The Platonic theory of night is explained in the Timaeus, Chap. xix.

[232] Plato (Phaed. S: 133) makes the same comparison. Eti toinon, ephe, pammega te einai auto, kai hemas oikein tous mechri Erakleion stelon apo Phasidos en smikro tini mori& 251; hosper peri telma murmekas e batrachous peri ten thalattan oikountas. Fialon names Seneca (Quaest. Nat. i. praef. 505) and Lucian (Hermotimus v. and Icaromenippus xix.) as following him. To these may be added Celsus "katagelon to 'Ioudaion kai Christianon genos" in Origen, C. Cels iv. 517, B.

The Haxaemeron - St Basil

intersected by valleys as rounded and smooth, because it reaches only to the salient parts, and is not able, on account of its weakness, to penetrate into the valleys which separate them. It does not even preserve the form of objects, and thinks that all square towers are round. Thus all proves that at a great distance sight only presents to us obscure and confused objects. The luminary is then great, according to the witness of Scripture, and infinitely greater than it appears.

10. See again another evident proof of its greatness. Although the heaven may be full of stars without number, the light contributed by them all could not disperse the gloom of night. The sun alone, from the time that it appeared on the horizon, while it was still expected and had not yet risen completely above the earth, dispersed the darkness, outshone the stars, dissolved and diffused the air, which was hitherto thick and condensed over our heads, and produced thus the morning breeze and the dew which in fine weather streams over the earth. Could the earth with such a wide extent be lighted up entirely in one moment if an immense disc were not pouring forth its light over it? Recognise here the wisdom of the Artificer. See how He made the heat of the sun proportionate to this distance. Its heat is so regulated that it neither consumes the earth by excess, nor lets it grow cold and sterile by defect.

To all this the properties of the moon are near akin; she, too, has an immense body, whose splendour only yields to that of the sun. Our eyes, however, do not always see her in her full size. Now she presents a perfectly rounded disc, now when diminished and

The Haxaemeron - St Basil

lessened she shows a deficiency on one side. When waxing she is shadowed on one side, and when she is waning another side is hidden. Now it is not without a secret reason of the divine Maker of the universe, that the moon appears from time to time under such different forms. It presents a striking example of our nature. Nothing is stable in man; here from nothingness he raises himself to perfection; there after having hasted to put forth his strength to attain his full greatness he suddenly is subject to gradual deterioration, and is destroyed by diminution. Thus, the sight of the moon, making us think of the rapid vicissitudes of human things, ought to teach us not to pride ourselves on the good things of this life, and not to glory in our power, not to be carried away by uncertain riches, to despise our flesh which is subject to change, and to take care of the soul, for its good is unmoved. If you cannot behold without sadness the moon losing its splendour by gradual and imperceptible decrease, how much more distressed should you be at the sight of a soul, who, after having possessed virtue, loses its beauty by neglect, and does not remain constant to its affections, but is agitated and constantly changes because its purposes are unstable. What Scripture says is very true, "As for a fool he changeth as the moon."[233]

I believe also that the variations of the moon do not take place without exerting great influence upon the organization of animals and of all living things. This is because bodies are differently disposed at its waxing and waning. When she wanes they lose their density and become void. When she waxes and is

---

[233] Ecclus. xxvii. 11.

The Haxaemeron - St Basil

approaching her fulness they appear to fill themselves at the same time with her, thanks to an imperceptible moisture that she emits mixed with heat, which penetrates everywhere.[234] For proof, see how those who sleep under the moon feel abundant moisture filling their heads;[235] see how fresh meat is quickly turned under the action of the moon;[236] see the brain of animals, the moistest part of marine animals, the pith of trees. Evidently the moon must be, as Scripture says, of enormous size and power to make all nature thus participate in her changes.

---

[234] cf. Alcman (ap. Plut., Sympos. iii. 10) who calls the dew Dios thugater kai Selanas; and Plutarch himself in loc. Virg., Georg. iii. 337, "Roscida Luna," and Statius, Theb. i. 336: "Iamque per emeriti surgens confinia Phoebi Titanis, late mundo subvecta silenti Rorifera gelidum tenuaverat aera biga."

[235] The baleful influence of "iracunda Diana" (Hor., De Art. Poet. 454) is an early belief, not yet extinct. cf. the term seleniasmos for epilepsy, and "lunaticus" for the "moonstruck" madman. Vide Cass., Quaest. Med. xxv. 1. Perowne on Ps. cxxi. 6 notes, "De Wette refers to Andersen's Eastern Travels in proof that this opinion is commonly entertained. Delitzsch mentions having heard from Texas that the consequence of sleeping in the open air, when the moon was shining, was mental aberration, dizziness, and even death." "Dass auch der Mond in heller Nacht dem ohne gehoerigen Schutz Schlafenden schaden koenne ist allgemeine Meinung des Orients und der koehlen Naechte wegen leicht moeglich. Vgl. Carne Leben und Sitten im Morgenl.'" Ewald, Dichter des A.B. ii. 266.

[236] A fact, however explained. Plutarch (Sympos. Prob. iii. 10) discusses the question Dia ti ta krea sepetai mallon hupo ten selenen e ton helion, and refers the decomposition to the moistening influence of the moon. "Air, moisture, and a certain degree of warmth, are necessary to the decay of animal bodies...where moisture continues present—even though warmth and air be in a great measure excluded—decay still slowly takes place." J. F. W. Johnston, Chemistry of Common Life, ii. 273.

The Haxaemeron - St Basil

11. On its variations depends also the condition of the air, as is proved by sudden disturbances which often come after the new moon, in the midst of a calm and of a stillness in the winds, to agitate the clouds and to hurl them against each other; as the flux and reflux in straits, and the ebb and flow of the ocean prove, so that those who live on its shores see it regularly following the revolutions of the moon. The waters of straits approach and retreat from one shore to the other during the different phases of the moon; but, when she is new, they have not an instant of rest, and move in perpetual swaying to and fro, until the moon, reappearing, regulates their reflux. As to the Western sea,[237] we see it in its ebb and flow now return into its bed, and now overflow, as the moon draws it back by her respiration and then, by her expiration, urges it to its own boundaries.[238]

I have entered into these details, to show you the grandeur of the luminaries, and to make you see that, in the inspired words, there is not one idle syllable. And yet my sermon has scarcely touched on any important point; there are many other discoveries about the size and distance of the sun and moon to which any one who will make a serious study of their action and of their characteristics may arrive by the aid of reason. Let me then ingenuously make an avowal of my weakness, for fear that you should measure the mighty works of the Creator by my words. The little that I have said ought the rather to

---

[237] i.e. the Atlantic. cf. Ovid., Met. xi. 258, "Hesperium fretum."

[238] Pytheas, of Marseilles, is first named as attributing the tides to the moon. Plut. peri aresk. k.t.l. iii. 17. On the ancient belief generally vide Plin. ii. 99.

make you conjecture the marvels on which I have omitted to dwell. We must not then measure the moon with the eye, but with the reason. Reason, for the discovery of truth, is much surer than the eye.

Everywhere ridiculous old women's tales, imagined in the delirium of drunkenness, have been circulated; such as that enchantments can remove the moon from its place and make it descend to the earth. How could a magician's charm shake that of which the Most High has laid the foundations? And if once torn out what place could hold it?[239]

Do you wish from slight indications to have a proof of the moon's size? All the towns in the world, however distant from each other, equally receive the light from the moon in those streets that are turned towards its rising. If she did not look on all face to face, those only would be entirely lighted up which were exactly opposite; as to those beyond the extremities of her disc, they would only receive diverted and oblique rays. It is this effect which the light of lamps produces in houses; if a lamp is surrounded by several persons, only the shadow of the person who is directly opposite to it is cast in a straight line, the others follow inclined lines on each side. In the same way, if the body of the moon were not of an immense and prodigious size

---

[239] "Inventa jam pridem ratio est praenuntians horas, non modo dies ac noctes, Solis Lunaeque defectuum. Durat tamen tradita persuasio in magna parte vulgi, veneficiis et herbis id cogi, eamque num faeminarum scientiam praevalere." Plin. xxv. v. So it was a custom to avert the spells of sorceresses, which might bring the eclipsed moon to the ground, by beating brass and shouting. cf. Juv., Sat. vi. 443, "Tam nemo tubas, nemo oera fatigat, Una laboranti poterit succurrere lunae," and the "oera auxiliaria lunae" of Ov., Met. iv. 333.

she could not extend herself alike to all. In reality, when the moon rises in the equinoctial regions, all equally enjoy her light, both those who inhabit the icy zone, under the revolutions of the Bear, and those who dwell in the extreme south in the neighbourhood of the torrid zone. She gives us an idea of her size by appearing to be face to face with all people. Who then can deny the immensity of a body which divides itself equally over such a wide extent?

But enough on the greatness of the sun and moon. May He Who has given us intelligence to recognise in the smallest objects of creation the great wisdom of the Contriver make us find in great bodies a still higher idea of their Creator. However, compared with their Author, the sun and moon are but a fly and an ant. The whole universe cannot give us a right idea of the greatness of God; and it is only by signs, weak and slight in themselves, often by the help of the smallest insects and of the least plants, that we raise ourselves to Him. Content with these words let us offer our thanks, I to Him who has given me the ministry of the Word, you to Him who feeds you with spiritual food; Who, even at this moment, makes you find in my weak voice the strength of barley bread. May He feed you for ever, and in proportion to your faith grant you the manifestation of the Spirit[240] in Jesus Christ our Lord, to whom be glory and power for ever and ever. Amen.

---

[240] cf. 1 Cor. xii. 7.

Homily VII

The creation of moving creatures.[241]

1. "And God said, Let the waters bring forth abundantly the moving creature that hath life" after their kind, "and fowl that may fly above the earth" after their kind.[242] After the creation of the luminaries the waters are now filled with living beings and its own adornment is given to this part of the world. Earth had received hers from her own plants, the heavens had received the flowers of the stars, and, like two eyes, the great luminaries beautified them in concert. It still remained for the waters to receive their adornment. The command was given, and immediately the rivers and lakes becoming fruitful brought forth their natural broods; the sea travailed with all kinds of swimming creatures; not even in mud and marshes did the water remain idle; it took its part in creation. Everywhere from its ebullition frogs, gnats and flies came forth. For that which we see to-day is the sign of the past. Thus everywhere the water hastened to obey the Creator's command. Who could count the species which the great and ineffable power of God caused to be suddenly seen living and moving, when this command had empowered the waters to bring forth life? Let the waters bring forth moving creatures that have life. Then for the first time is made a being with life and feeling. For though plants and trees be said to live, seeing that they share the power of being nourished and growing; nevertheless they are neither

---

[241] LXX. creeping things.

[242] Gen. i. 20.

The Haxaemeron - St Basil

living beings, nor have they life.[243] To create these last God said, "Let the water produce moving creatures."

Every creature that swims, whether it skims on the surface of the waters, or cleaves the depths, is of the nature of a moving creature,[244] since it drags itself on the body of the water. Certain aquatic animals have feet and walk; especially amphibia, such as seals, crabs, crocodiles, river horses[245] and frogs; but they are above all gifted with the power of swimming. Thus it is said, Let the waters produce moving creatures. In these few words what species is omitted? Which is not included in the command of the Creator? Do we not see viviparous animals, seals, dolphins, rays and all cartilaginous animals? Do we not see oviparous animals comprising every sort of fish, those which have a skin and those which have scales, those which have fins and those which have not? This command has only required one word, even less than a word, a sign, a motion of the divine will, and it has such a wide sense that it includes all the varieties and all the families of fish. To review them all would be to undertake to count the waves of the ocean or to measure its waters in the hollow of the hand. "Let the waters produce moving creatures." That is to say, those which people the high seas and those which love the shores; those which inhabit the depths and those which attach themselves to rocks; those which are gregarious and those which live dispersed, the

---

[243] Plants are neither zoa nor empsucha.

[244] LXX. creeping.

[245] Basil uses the classical greek form hoi potamioi hippoi, as in Herod. and Arist. The dog-Greek hippopotamus, properly a horse-river, is first found in Galen.

The Haxaemeron - St Basil

cetaceous, the huge, and the tiny. It is from the same power, the same command, that all, small and great receive their existence. "Let the waters bring forth." These words show you the natural affinity of animals which swim in the water; thus, fish, when drawn out of the water, quickly die, because they have no respiration such as could attract our air and water is their element, as air is that of terrestrial animals. The reason for it is clear. With us the lung, that porous and spongy portion of the inward parts which receives air by the dilatation of the chest, disperses and cools interior warmth; in fish the motion of the gills, which open and shut by turns to take in and to eject the water, takes the place of respiration.[246] Fish have a peculiar lot, a special nature, a nourishment of their own, a life apart. Thus they cannot be tamed and cannot bear the touch of a man's hand.[247]

---

[246] cf. Arist., De Part. Anim. iii. 6. dioper ton men ichthuon oudeis echei pneumona all' anti toutou branchia kathaper eiretai en tois peri anapnoes; hudati gar poieitai ten katapsuxin, ta d' anapneonta echei pneumona anapnei de ta peza panta.

[247] Here Basil is curiously in contradiction to ancient as well as modern experience. Martial's epigram on Domitian's tame fish, "qui norunt dominum, manumque lambunt illam qua nihil est in orbe majus" (iv. 30) is illustrated by the same author's "natat ad magistrum delicata muraena" (x. 30), as well as by AElian (De animal. viii. 4). "Apud Baulos in parte Baiana piscinam habuit Hortensius orator, in qua muraenam adeo dilexit ut exanimatam flesse credatur: in eadem villa Antonia Drusi muraenae quam diligebat inaures addidit." Plin. ix. 71. So Lucian houtoi de (ichthues) kai onomata echousi kai erchontai kaloumenoi. (De Syr. Dea. 45.) John Evelyn (Dairy 1644) writes of Fontainebleau: "The carps come familiarly to hand." There was recently a tame carp at Azay le Rideau.

The Haxaemeron - St Basil

2. "Let the waters bring forth moving creatures after their kind." God caused to be born the firstlings of each species to serve as seeds for nature. Their multitudinous numbers are kept up in subsequent succession, when it is necessary for them to grow and multiply. Of another kind is the species of testacea, as muscles, scallops, sea snails, conches, and the infinite variety of oysters. Another kind is that of the crustacea, as crabs and lobsters; another of fish without shells, with soft and tender flesh, like polypi and cuttle fish. And amidst these last what an innumerable variety! There are weevers, lampreys and eels, produced in the mud of rivers and ponds, which more resemble venomous reptiles than fish in their nature. Of another kind is the species of the ovipara; of another, that of the vivipara. Among the latter are sword-fish, cod, in one word, all cartilaginous fish, and even the greater part of the cetacea, as dolphins, seals, which, it is said, if they see their little ones, still quite young, frightened, take them back into their belly to protect them.[248]

Let the waters bring forth after their kind. The species of the cetacean is one; another is that of small fish. What infinite variety in the different kinds! All have their own names, different food, different form, shape, and quality of flesh. All present infinite variety, and are divided into innumerable classes. Is there a tunny fisher who can enumerate to us the different varieties of that fish? And yet they tell us that at the sight of great swarms of fish they can almost tell the number of the individual ones which compose it. What man is there of all that have spent their long lives by coasts

---

[248] Narrated by AElian (Anim i. 16) of the "glaucus," a fish apparently unknown.

The Haxaemeron - St Basil

and shores, who can inform us with exactness of the history of all fish?

Some are known to the fishermen of the Indian ocean, others to the toilers of the Egyptian gulf, others to the islanders, others to the men of Mauretania.[249] Great and small were all alike created by this first command, by this ineffable power. What a difference in their food! What a variety in the manner in which each species reproduces itself! Most fish do not hatch eggs like birds; they do not build nests; they do not feed their young with toil; it is the water which receives and vivifies the egg dropped into it. With them the reproduction of each species is invariable, and natures are not mixed. There are none of those unions which, on the earth, produce mules and certain birds contrary to the nature of their species. With fish there is no variety which, like the ox and the sheep, is armed with a half-equipment of teeth, none which ruminates except, according to certain writers, the scar.[250] All have serried and very sharp teeth, for fear their food should escape them if they masticate it for too long a time. In fact, if it were not crushed and swallowed as soon as divided, it would be carried away by the water.

3. The food of fish differs according to their species. Some feed on mud; others eat sea weed; others content themselves with the herbs that grow in water. But the greater part devour each other, and the smaller is food for the larger, and if one which has possessed itself of a fish weaker than itself becomes

---

[249] Maurousioi. cf. Strabo, ii. 33.

[250] e.g. Arist., De Anim. viii. 2 and AElian, ii. 54.

a prey to another, the conqueror and the conquered are both swallowed up in the belly of the last. And we mortals, do we act otherwise when we press our inferiors?[251] What difference is there between the last fish and the man who, impelled by devouring greed, swallows the weak in the folds of his insatiable avarice? Yon fellow possessed the goods of the poor; you caught him and made him a part of your abundance. You have shown yourself more unjust than the unjust, and more miserly than the miser. Look to it lest you end like the fish, by hook, by weel, or by net. Surely we too, when we have done the deeds of the wicked, shall not escape punishment at the last.

Now see what tricks, what cunning, are to be found in a weak animal, and learn not to imitate wicked doers. The crab loves the flesh of the oyster; but, sheltered by its shell, a solid rampart with which nature has furnished its soft and delicate flesh, it is a difficult prey to seize. Thus they call the oyster "sherd-hide."[252] Thanks to the two shells with which it is enveloped, and which adapt themselves perfectly the one to the other, the claws of the crab are quite powerless. What does he do? When he sees it, sheltered from the wind, warming itself with pleasure, and half opening

---

[251] cf. Pericles ii. i. 3 Fish. Master, I marvel how the fishes live in the sea. 1 Fish. Why, as men do a-land; the great ones eat up the little ones.

[252] ostrakodermos.

The Haxaemeron - St Basil

its shells to the sun,[253] he secretly throws in a pebble, prevents them from closing, and takes by cunning what force had lost.[254] Such is the malice of these animals, deprived as they are of reason and of speech. But I would that you should at once rival the crab in cunning and industry, and abstain from harming your neighbour; this animal is the image of him who craftily approaches his brother, takes advantage of his neighbour's misfortunes, and finds his delight in other men's troubles. O copy not the damned! Content yourself with your own lot. Poverty, with what is necessary, is of more value in the eyes of the wise than all pleasures.

I will not pass in silence the cunning and trickery of the squid, which takes the colour of the rock to which it attaches itself. Most fish swim idly up to the squid as they might to a rock, and become themselves the prey of the crafty creature.[255] Such are men who court ruling powers, bending themselves to all circumstances and not remaining for a moment in the same purpose; who praise self-restraint in the

---

[253] Fialon quotes Le Fontaine Le Rat et l'Huitre: Parmi tant d'huitres toutes closes, Une s'etait ouverte, et baillant au soleil, Par un doux Zephyr rejouie, Humait l'air, respirait etait epanouie, Blanche, grasse, et d'un gout, `a la voir, sans pareil.

[254] Pliny ix. 48, says of the octopus: "imposito lapillo extra corpus ne palpitatu ejiciatur: ita securi grassantur, extrahuntque carnes."

[255] cf. Theog. 215: poulupou orgen ische poluplokou, hos poti petre te prosomilesei toios idein ephane Nun men tes ephepou, pote d'alloios chroa gignou, kraipnon toi sophie gignetai eutropies . Greg. Naz., Or. xxxvi.: pollas metalambanon chroas hosper ta ton petron hei polupodes hais han homilesosi, and Arist., Hist. An. ix. 37: kai thereuei tous ichthus to chroma metaballon kai poion homoion hois de plesiaze lithois.

The Haxaemeron - St Basil

company of the self-restrained, and license in that of the licentious, accommodating their feelings to the pleasure of each. It is difficult to escape them and to put ourselves on guard against their mischief; because it is under the mask of friendship that they hide their clever wickedness. Men like this are ravening wolves covered with sheep's clothing, as the Lord calls them.[256] Flee then fickleness and pliability; seek truth, sincerity, simplicity. The serpent is shifty; so he has been condemned to crawl. The just is an honest man, like Job.[257] Wherefore God setteth the solitary in families.[258] So is this great and wide sea, wherein are things creeping innumerable, both small and great beasts.[259] Yet a wise and marvellous order reigns among these animals. Fish do not always deserve our reproaches; often they offer us useful examples. How is it that each sort of fish, content with the region that has been assigned to it, never travels over its own limits to pass into foreign seas? No surveyor has ever distributed to them their habitations, nor enclosed them in walls, nor assigned limits to them; each kind has been naturally assigned its own home. One gulf nourishes one kind of fish, another other sorts; those which swarm here are absent elsewhere. No mountain raises its sharp

---

[256] cf. Matt. vii. 15.

[257] So the Cod. Colb. and Eustathius, who renders Justus nihil habet fictum sicut Job. The Ben. Ed. suspect that Basil wrote Jacob and Job. Four mss. support Jacob alone, who, whatever may be the meaning of the Hebrew in Gen. xxv. 27, is certainly aplastos only in the LXX., and a bad instance of guilelessness.

[258] Ps. lxviii. 6.

[259] Ps. civ. 25.

peaks between them; no rivers bar the passage to them; it is a law of nature, which according to the

The Haxaemeron - St Basil

needs of each kind, has allotted to them their dwelling

places with equality and justice.[260]

---

[260] cf. Cudworth, Int. Syst. iii. 37, 23: "Besides this plastick Nature which is in animals, forming their several bodies artificially, as so many microcosms or little worlds, there must also be a general plastick Nature in the macrocosm, the whole corporeal universe, that which makes all things thus to conspire everywhere, and agree together into one harmony. Concerning which plastick nature of the universe, the Author De Mundo writes after this manner, kai ton holon kosmon, diekosmese mia he dia panton diekousa dunamis, one power, passing through all things, ordered and formed the whole world. Again he calls the same pneuma kai empsuchon kai gonimon ousian, a spirit, and a living and Generative Nature, and plainly declares it to be a thing distinct from the Deity, but subordinate to it and dependent on it. But Aristotle himself, in that genuine work of his before mentioned, speaks clearly and positively concerning the Plastick Nature of the Universe, as well as that of animals, in these words: It seemeth that as there is Art in Artificial things, so in the things of Nature, there is another such like Principle or Cause, which we ourselves partake of: in the same manner as we do of Heat and Cold, from the Universe. Wherefore it is more probable that the whole world was at first made by such a cause as this (if at least it were made) and that it is still conserved by the same, than mortal animals should be so: for there is much more of order and determinate Regularity in the Heavenly Bodies that in ourselves; but more of Fortuitousness and inconstant Regularity among these mortal things. Notwithstanding which, some there are, who though they cannot but acknowledge that the Bodies of Animals were all framed by an Artificial Nature, yet they will need contend that the System of the Heavens sprung merely from Fortune and Chance; although there be not the least appearance of Fortuitousness or Temerity in it.' And then he sums up all into this conclusion: hoste einai phaneron hoti esti ti toiouton ho de kai kaloumen phusin. Wherefore it is manifest that there is some such thing as that which we call Nature,' that is, that there is not only an Artificial,' Methodical,' and Plastick Nature in Animals, by which their respective Bodies are Framed and Conserved, but also that there is such a General Plastick Nature likewise in the

The Haxaemeron - St Basil

4. It is not thus with us. Why? Because we incessantly move the ancient landmarks which our fathers have set.[261] We encroach, we add house to house, field to field, to enrich ourselves at the expense of our neighbour. The great fish know the sojourning place that nature has assigned to them; they occupy the sea far from the haunts of men, where no islands lie, and where are no continents rising to confront them, because it has never been crossed and neither curiosity nor need has persuaded sailors to tempt it. The monsters that dwell in this sea are in size like high mountains, so witnesses who have seen tell us, and never cross their boundaries to ravage islands and seaboard towns. Thus each kind is as if it were stationed in towns, in villages, in an ancient country, and has for its dwelling place the regions of the sea which have been assigned to it.

Instances have, however, been known of migratory fish, who, as if common deliberation transported them into strange regions, all start on their march at a given sign. When the time marked for breeding arrives, they, as if awakened by a common law of nature, migrate from gulf to gulf, directing their course toward the North Sea. And at the epoch of their return you may see all these fish streaming like a torrent across the Propontis towards the Euxine Sea. Who puts them in marching array? Where is the prince's order? Has an edict affixed in the public place indicated to them their day of departure? Who serves them as a guide? See how the divine order embraces all and extends to the smallest object. A fish does not resist God's law, and we men cannot endure His precepts of salvation! Do

---

[261] cf. Prov. xxii. 28.

The Haxaemeron - St Basil

not despise fish because they are dumb and quite unreasoning; rather fear lest, in your resistance to the disposition of the Creator, you have even less reason than they. Listen to the fish, who by their actions all but speak and say: it is for the perpetuation of our race that we undertake this long voyage. They have not the gift of reason, but they have the law of nature firmly seated within them, to show them what they have to do. Let us go, they say, to the North Sea. Its water is sweeter than that of the rest of the sea; for the sun does not remain long there, and its rays do not draw up all the drinkable portions.[262] Even sea creatures love fresh water.[263] Thus one often sees them enter into rivers and swim far up them from the sea. This is the reason which makes them prefer the Euxine Sea to other gulfs, as the most fit for breeding and for bringing up their young. When they have obtained their object the whole tribe returns home. Let us hear these dumb creatures tell us the reason. The Northern sea, they say, is shallow and its surface is exposed to the violence of the wind, and it has few shores and retreats. Thus the winds easily agitate it to its bottom and mingle the sands of its bed with its waves. Besides, it is cold in winter, filled as it is from all directions by large rivers. Wherefore after a moderate enjoyment of its waters, during the summer, when the winter comes they hasten to reach warmer depths and places heated by the sun, and after fleeing from the stormy tracts of the North, they seek a haven in less agitated seas.

---

[262] cf. Arist., Hist. Animal. viii. 12 and 13, and note on p. 70.

[263] cf. Arist. and Theophrastus.

The Haxaemeron - St Basil

5. I myself have seen these marvels, and I have admired the wisdom of God in all things. If beings deprived of reason are capable of thinking and of providing for their own preservation; if a fish knows what it ought to seek and what to shun, what shall we say, who are honoured with reason, instructed by law, encouraged by the promises, made wise by the Spirit, and are nevertheless less reasonable about our own affairs than the fish? They know how to provide for the future, but we renounce our hope of the future and spend our life in brutal indulgence. A fish traverses the extent of the sea to find what is good for it; what will you say then—you who live in idleness, the mother of all vices?[264] Do not let any one make his ignorance an excuse. There has been implanted in us natural reason which tells us to identify ourselves with good, and to avoid all that is harmful. I need not go far from the sea to find examples, as that is the object of our researches. I have heard it said by one living near the sea, that the sea urchin, a little contemptible creature, often foretells calm and tempest to sailors. When it foresees a disturbance of the winds, it gets under a great pebble, and clinging to it as to an anchor, it tosses about in safety, retained by the weight which prevents it from becoming the plaything of the waves.[265] It is a certain sign for sailors that they are threatened with a violent agitation of the winds. No

---

[264] Otiosa mater est nugarum noverca omnium virtutum. St. Bernard.

[265] "Tradunt saevitiam maris praesagire eos, correptisque opperiri lapillis, mobilitatem pondere stabilientes: nolunt volutatione spinas atterere, quod ubi videre nautici, statim pluribus ancoris navigia infraenant." Plin. ix. 5. cf. Plut., De Solert. An. 979, Oppian, Halieut. ii. 225, and AElian, Hist. An. vii. 33.

astrologer, no Chaldaean, reading in the rising of the stars the disturbances of the air, has ever communicated his secret to the urchin: it is the Lord of the sea and of the winds who has impressed on this little animal a manifest proof of His great wisdom. God has foreseen all, He has neglected nothing. His eye, which never sleeps, watches over all.[266] He is present everywhere and gives to each being the means of preservation. If God has not left the sea urchin outside His providence, is He without care for you?

"Husbands love your wives."[267] Although formed of two bodies you are united to live in the communion of wedlock. May this natural link, may this yoke imposed by the blessing, reunite those who are divided. The viper, the cruelest of reptiles, unites itself with the sea lamprey, and, announcing its presence by a hiss, it calls it from the depths to conjugal union. The lamprey obeys, and is united to this venomous animal.[268] What does this mean? However hard, however fierce a husband may be, the wife ought to bear with him, and not wish to find any pretext for breaking the union. He strikes you, but he is your husband. He is a drunkard, but he is united to you by nature. He is brutal and

---

[266] cf. Prov. xv. 3: "The eyes of the Lord are in every place," and Ps. cxxi. 3. So Hesiod, panta idon Dios ophthalmos kai panta noesas. Hes. Works and Days, 265.

[267] Eph. v. 25.

[268] The fable is in AElian, Hist. An. ix. 66, and is contradicted by Athenaeus, who says (vii. p. 312): 'Andreas de en to peri ton pseudos pepisteumenon pseudos phesin einai to Murainan echii mignusthai proserchomenen epi to tenagodes, oude gar epi tenagous echeis nemesthai, philedountas limodesin eremiais. Sostratos de en tois peri Zoon sunkatatithetai te mixei.

The Haxaemeron - St Basil

cross, but he is henceforth one of your members, and the most precious of all.

6. Let husbands listen as well: here is a lesson for them. The viper vomits forth its venom in respect for marriage; and you, will you not put aside the barbarity and the inhumanity of your soul, out of respect for your union? Perhaps the example of the viper contains another meaning. The union of the viper and of the lamprey is an adulterous violation of nature. You, who are plotting against other men's wedlock, learn what creeping creature you are like. I have only one object, to make all I say turn to the edification of the Church. Let then libertines put a restraint on their passions, for they are taught by the examples set by creatures of earth and sea.

My bodily infirmity and the lateness of the hour force me to end my discourse. However, I have still many observations to make on the products of the sea, for the admiration of my attentive audience. To speak of the sea itself, how does its water change into salt? How is it that coral, a stone so much esteemed, is a plant in the midst of the sea, and when once exposed to the air becomes hard as a rock? Why has nature enclosed in the meanest of animals, in an oyster, so precious an object as a pearl? For these pearls, which are coveted by the caskets of kings, are cast upon the shores, upon the coasts, upon sharp rocks, and enclosed in oyster shells. How can the sea pinna produce her fleece of gold, which no dye has ever

The Haxaemeron - St Basil

imitated?[269] How can shells give kings purple of a brilliancy not surpassed by the flowers of the field?

"Let the waters bring forth." What necessary object was there that did not immediately appear? What object of luxury was not given to man? Some to supply his needs, some to make him contemplate the marvels of creation. Some are terrible, so as to take our idleness to school. "God created great whales."[270] Scripture gives them the name of "great" not because they are greater than a shrimp and a sprat, but because the size of their bodies equals that of great hills. Thus when they swim on the surface of the waters one often sees them appear like islands. But these monstrous creatures do not frequent our coasts and shores; they inhabit the Atlantic ocean. Such are these animals created to strike us with terror and awe. If now you hear say that the greatest vessels, sailing with full sails, are easily stopped by a very small fish, by the remora, and so forcibly that the ship remains motionless for a long time, as if it had taken root in the

---

[269] The Pinna is a bivalve with a silky beard, of which several species are found in the Mediterranean. The beard is called by modern naturalists byssus. The shell of the giant pinna is sometimes two feet long.

[270] Gen. i. 21.

The Haxaemeron - St Basil

middle of the sea,[271] do you not see in this little creature a like proof of the power of the Creator? Sword fish, saw fish, dog fish, whales, and sharks, are not therefore the only things to be dreaded; we have to fear no less the spike of the stingray even after its death, [272] and the sea-hare, [273] whose mortal blows are as rapid as they are inevitable. Thus the Creator wishes that all may keep you awake, so that full of hope in Him you may avoid the evils with which all these creatures threaten you.

But let us come out of the depths of the sea and take refuge upon the shore. For the marvels of creation, coming one after the other in constant succession like the waves, have submerged my discourse. However, I should not be surprised if, after finding greater wonders upon the earth, my spirit seeks like Jonah's to flee to the sea. But it seems to me, that meeting with these innumerable marvels has made me forget all measure, and experience the fate of those who

---

[271] "Tamen omnia haec, pariterque eodem impellentia unus ac parvus admodum pisciculus, echeneis appellatus, in se tenet. Ruant venti licet, et saeviant procellae imperat furori, viresque tantas compescit, et cogit stare navigia: quod non vincula ulla, non anchorae pondere, irrevocabili jactae...Fertur Actiaco marte tenuisse navim Antonii properantis circumire et exhortare suos donec transiret in aliam....Tennit et nostra memoria Caii principis ab Astura Antium renavigantes." Plin. xxxii. 1. The popular error was long lived. "Life is a voyage, and, in our life's ways, Countries, courts, towns, are rocks or remoras." Donne, To Sir Henry Wotton.

[272] Pliny (ix. 72) says it is sometimes five inches long. AElian (Hist. An. i. 56) calls the wound incurable.

[273] Pliny (ix. 72) calls it tactu pestilens, and says (xxxii. 3) that no other fish eats it, except the mullet.

The Haxaemeron - St Basil

navigate the high seas without a fixed point to mark their progress, and are often ignorant of the space which they have traversed. This is what has happened to me; whilst my words glanced at creation, I have not been sensible of the multitude of beings of which I spoke to you. But although this honourable assembly is pleased by my speech, and the recital of the marvels of the Master is grateful to the ears of His servants, let me here bring the ship of my discourse to anchor, and await the day to deliver you the rest. Let us, therefore, all arise, and, giving thanks for what has been said, let us ask for strength to hear the rest. Whilst taking your food may the conversation at your table turn upon what has occupied us this morning and this evening. Filled with these thoughts may you, even in sleep, enjoy the pleasure of the day, so that you may be permitted to say, "I sleep but my heart waketh,"[274] meditating day and night upon the law of the Lord, to Whom be glory and power world without end. Amen.

---

[274] Cant. v. 2.

The Haxaemeron - St Basil

Homily VIII

The creation of fowl and water animals.[275]

1. And God said "Let the earth bring forth the living creature after his kind, cattle and creeping things, and beast of the earth after his kind; and it was so."[276] The command of God advanced step by step and earth thus received her adornment. Yesterday it was said, "Let the waters produce moving things," and to-day "let the earth bring forth the living creature." Is the earth then alive? And are the mad-minded Manichaeans right in giving it a soul? At these words "Let the earth bring forth," it did not produce a germ contained in it, but He who gave the order at the same time gifted it with the grace and power to bring forth. When the earth had heard this command "Let the earth bring forth grass and the tree yielding fruit," it was not grass that it had hidden in it that it caused to spring forth, it did not bring to the surface a palm tree, an oak, a cypress, hitherto kept back in its depths. It is the word of God which forms the nature of things created. "Let the earth bring forth;" that is to say not that she may bring forth that which she has but that she may acquire that which she lacks, when God gives her the power. Even so now, "Let the earth bring forth the living creature," not the living creature that is contained in herself, but that which the command of God gives her. Further, the Manichaeans contradict themselves, because if the earth has

---

[275] Codex Colb. 1 has the title "about creeping things and beasts."

[276] Gen. i. 24.

The Haxaemeron - St Basil

brought forth the life, she has left herself despoiled of life. Their execrable doctrine needs no demonstration.

But why did the waters receive the command to bring forth the moving creature that hath life and the earth to bring forth the living creature? We conclude that, by their nature, swimming creatures appear only to have an imperfect life, because they live in the thick element of water. They are hard of hearing, and their sight is dull because they see through the water; they have no memory, no imagination, no idea of social intercourse. Thus divine language appears to indicate that, in aquatic animals, the carnal life originates their psychic movements, whilst in terrestrial animals, gifted with a more perfect life,[277] the soul[278] enjoys supreme authority. In fact the greater part of quadrupeds have more power of penetration in their senses; their apprehension of present objects is keen, and they keep all exact remembrance of the past. It seems therefore, that God, after the command given to the waters to bring forth moving creatures that have life, created simply living bodies for aquatic animals, whilst for terrestrial animals He commanded the soul to exist and to direct the body, showing thus that the inhabitants of the earth are gifted with greater vital force. Without doubt terrestrial animals are devoid of reason. At the same time how many affections of the soul each one of them expresses by the voice of nature! They express by cries their joy and sadness, recognition of what is familiar to them, the need of food, regret at being separated from their companions, and numberless emotions. Aquatic

---

[277] zoe.

[278] psuche.

animals, on the contrary, are not only dumb; it is impossible to tame them, to teach them, to train them for man's society.[279] "The ox knoweth his owner, and the ass his master's crib."[280] But the fish does not know who feeds him. The ass knows a familiar voice, he knows the road which he has often trodden, and even, if man loses his way, he sometimes serves him as a guide. His hearing is more acute than that of any other terrestrial animal. What animal of the sea can show so much rancour and resentment as the camel? The camel conceals its resentment for a long time after it has been struck, until it finds an opportunity, and then repays the wrong. Listen, you whose heart does not pardon, you who practise vengeance as a virtue; see what you resemble when you keep your anger for so long against your neighbour like a spark, hidden in the ashes, and only waiting for fuel to set your heart ablaze!

2. "Let the earth bring forth a living soul." Why did the earth produce a living soul? so that you may make a difference between the soul of cattle and that of man. You will soon learn how the human soul was formed; hear now about the soul of creatures devoid of reason. Since, according to Scripture, "the life of every creature is in the blood,"[281] as the blood when thickened changes into flesh, and flesh when corrupted decomposes into earth, so the soul of beasts is naturally an earthy substance. "Let the earth bring forth a living soul." See the affinity of the soul

---

[279] See note on p. 90.

[280] Isa. i. 3.

[281] cf. Lev. xvii. 11.

with blood, of blood with flesh, of flesh with earth; and remounting in an inverse sense from the earth to the flesh, from the flesh to the blood, from the blood to the soul, you will find that the soul of beasts is earth. Do not suppose that it is older than the essence[282] of their body, nor that it survives the dissolution of the flesh;[283] avoid the nonsense of those arrogant philosophers who do not blush to liken their soul to that of a dog; who say that they have been formerly themselves women, shrubs, fish.[284] Have they ever been fish? I do not know; but I do not fear to affirm that in their writings they show less sense than fish. "Let the earth bring forth the living creature." Perhaps many of you ask why there is such a long silence in the middle of the rapid rush of my discourse. The

---

[282] hupostasis.

[283] It may be supposed "that the souls of brutes, being but so many eradiations or effuxes from that source of life above, are, as soon as ever those organized bodies of theirs, by reason of their indisposition, become uncapable of being further acted upon by them, then to be resumed again and retracted back to their original head and fountain. Since it cannot be doubted but what creates anything out of nothing, or sends it forth from itself, by free and voluntary emanation, may be able either to retract the same back again to its original source, or else to annihilate it at pleasure. And I find that there have not wanted some among the Gentile philosophers themselves who have entertained this opinion, whereof Porphyry is one, luetai hekaste dunamis alogos eis ten holen zoen tou pantos." Cudworth, i. 35.

[284] Empedocles is named as author of the lines: ede gar pot' ego genomen kourete koros te, Thamnos t' oionos te kai ein hali ellopos ichthus cf. Diog. Laert. viii. 78, and Plutarch, D Solert. An. ii. 964. Whether the "faba Pythagorae cognata" of Hor., Sat. ii. 6, 63, implies the transmigration of the soul into it is doubtful. cf. Juv., Sat. xv. 153. Anaximander thought that human beings were originally generated from fish. Plut., Symp. viii. 8.

The Haxaemeron - St Basil

more studious among my auditors will not be ignorant of the reason why words fail me. What! Have I not seen them look at each other, and make signs to make me look at them, and to remind me of what I have passed over? I have forgotten a part of the creation, and that one of the most considerable, and my discourse was almost finished without touching upon it. "Let the waters bring forth abundantly the moving creature that hath life and fowl that may fly above the earth in the open firmament, of heaven."[285] I spoke of fish as long as eventide allowed: to-day we have passed to the examination of terrestrial animals; between the two, birds have escaped us. We are forgetful like travellers who unmindful of some important object, are obliged, although they be far on their road, to retrace their steps, punished for their negligence by the weariness of the journey. So we have to turn back. That which we have omitted is not to be despised. It is the third part of the animal creation, if indeed there are three kinds of animals, land, winged and water.

"Let the waters" it is said "bring forth abundantly moving creature that hath life and fowl that may fly above the earth in the open firmament of heaven." Why do the waters give birth also to birds? Because there is, so to say, a family link between the creatures that fly and those that swim. In the same way that fish cut the waters, using their fins to carry them forward and their tails to direct their movements round and round and straightforward, so we see birds float in the air by the help of their wings. Both endowed with the property of swimming, their common derivation from

---

[285] Gen. i. 20.

The Haxaemeron - St Basil

the waters has made them of one family.[286] At the same time no bird is without feet, because finding all its food upon the earth it cannot do without their service. Rapacious birds have pointed claws to enable them to close on their prey; to the rest has been given the indispensable ministry of feet to seek their food and to provide for the other needs of life. There are a few who walk badly, whose feet are neither suitable for walking nor for preying. Among this number are swallows, incapable of walking and seeking their prey, and the birds called swifts[287] who live on little insects carried about by the air. As to the swallow, its flight, which grazes the earth, fulfils the function of feet.

3. There are also innumerable kinds of birds. If we review them all, as we have partly done the fish, we shall find that under one name, the creatures which fly differ infinitely in size, form and colour; that in their life, their actions and their manners, they present a variety equally beyond the power of description. Thus some have tried to imagine names for them of which the singularity and the strangeness might, like brands,

---

[286] Fialon quotes Bossuet, 1st Elev. 5th week: "Qui a donne aux oiseaux et aux poissons ces rames naturelles, qui leur font fendre les eaux et les airs? Ce qui peut etre a donne lieu `a leur Createur de les produire ensemble, comme animaux d'un dessin `a peu pres semblable: le vol des oiseaux semblant, etre une espece de faculte de nager dans une liqueur plus subtile, comme la faculte de nager dans les poissons est une espece de vol dans une liqueur plus epaisse." The theory of evolutionists is, as is well known, that birds developed out of reptiles and reptiles from fish. Vide E. Haeckel's monophyletic pedigree in his History of Creation.

[287] drepanis, i.e. sickle-bird.

mark the distinctive character of each kind known. Some, as eagles, have been called Schizoptera, others Dermoptera, as the bats, others Ptilota, as wasps, others Coleoptera, as beetles and all those insects which brought forth in cases and coverings, break their prison to fly away in liberty.[288] But we have enough words of common usage to characterise each species and to mark the distinction which Scripture sets up between clean and unclean birds. Thus the species of carnivora is of one sort and of one constitution which suits their manner of living, sharp talons, curved beak, swift wings, allowing them to swoop easily upon their prey and to tear it up after having seized it.[289] The constitution of those who pick up seeds is different, and again that of those who live on all they come across. What a variety in all these creatures! Some are gregarious, except the birds of prey who know no other society than conjugal union; but innumerable kinds, doves, cranes, starlings, jackdaws, like a common life.[290] Among them some live without a chief and in a sort of independence; others, as cranes, do not refuse to submit themselves to a leader. And a fresh difference between them is that some are stationary and non-migratory; others undertake long voyages and the greater part of them migrate at the approach of winter. Nearly all birds can be tamed and are capable of training, except the weakest, who through fear and timidity cannot bear the constant and annoying contact of the hand. Some like the society of man and inhabit our dwellings;

---

[288] These are the terms of Aristotle, Hist. An. i. 5.

[289] cf. Arist., Hist. An. viii. 3.

[290] Whence the proverb koloios poti koloion. Arist., Eth. Nic. I. viii. 6.

The Haxaemeron - St Basil

others delight in mountains and in desert places. There is a great difference too in their peculiar notes. Some twitter and chatter, others are silent, some have a melodious and sonorous voice, some are wholly inharmonious and incapable of song; some imitate the voice of man, taught their mimicry either by nature or training;[291] others always give forth the same monotonous cry. The cock is proud; the peacock is vain of his beauty; doves and fowls are amorous, always seeking each other's society. The partridge is deceitful and jealous, lending perfidious help to the huntsmen to seize their prey.[292]

4. What a variety, I have said, in the actions and lives of flying creatures. Some of these unreasoning creatures even have a government, if the feature of government is to make the activity of all the individuals centre in one common end. This may be observed in bees. They have a common dwelling place; they fly in the air together, they work at the same work together; and what is still more extraordinary is that they give themselves to these labours under the guidance of a king and superintendent, and that they do not allow themselves to fly to the meadows without seeing if the king is flying at their head. As to this king, it is not election that gives him this authority; ignorance on the part of the people often puts the worst man in power; it is not fate; the blind decisions of fate often give authority to the most unworthy. It is not heredity that places him on the throne; it is only too common to see the

---

[291] "Super omnia humanas voces reddunt, posittaci quidem sermocinantes." Plin. x. 53.

[292] Arist., Hist. An. ix. 10.

The Haxaemeron - St Basil

children of kings, corrupted by luxury and flattery, living in ignorance of all virtue. It is nature which makes the king of the bees, for nature gives him superior size, beauty, and sweetness of character. He has a sting like the others, but he does not use it to revenge himself.[293] It is a principle of natural and unwritten law, that those who are raised to high office, ought to be lenient in punishing. Even bees who do not follow the example of their king, repent without delay of their imprudence, since they lose their lives with their sting. Listen, Christians, you to whom it is forbidden to "recompense evil for evil" and commanded "to overcome evil with good."[294] Take the bee for your model, which constructs its cells without injuring any one and without interfering with the goods of others. It gathers openly wax from the flowers with its mouth, drawing in the honey scattered over them like dew, and injects it into the hollow of its cells. Thus at first honey is liquid; time thickens it and gives it its

---

[293] Arist., Hist. An. v. 21, and Plin. xi. 17. "Ecce in re parva, villisque nostra annexa, cujus assidua copia est, non constat inter auctores, rex nullumne solus habeat aculeum, majestate tantum armatus: an dederit eum quidem natura, sed usum ejus illi tantum negaverit. Illud constat imperatorem aculeo non uti."

[294] Rom. xii. 17, 21.

The Haxaemeron - St Basil

sweetness.[295] The book of Proverbs has given the bee the most honourable and the best praise by calling her wise and industrious.[296] How much activity she exerts in gathering this precious nourishment, by which both kings and men of low degree are brought to health! How great is the art and cunning she displays in the construction of the store houses which are destined to receive the honey! After having spread the wax like a thin membrane, she distributes it in contiguous compartments which, weak though they are, by their number and by their mass, sustain the whole edifice. Each cell in fact holds to the one next to it, and is separated by a thin partition; we thus see two or three galleries of cells built one upon the other. The bee takes care not to make one vast cavity, for fear it might break under the weight of the liquid, and allow it to escape. See how the discoveries of geometry are mere by-works to the wise bee![297]

---

[295] The ancient belief was that honey fell from heaven, in the shape of dew, and the bee only gathered it from leaves. So Verg., Ec. iv. 30, "roscida mella," and Georg. iv. 1, "aerii mellis coelestia dona." cf. Arist., H. A. v. 22 meli de to pipton ek tou a& 153;ros, kai malista ton astron anatolais, kai hotan kataskephe he iris, and Plin. xi. 12. "Sive ille est coeli sudor, sive quaedam siderum saliva, sine purgantis se aeris succus,... magnam tamen coelestis naturae voluptatem affert." So Coleridge (Kubla Khan): "For he on honey dew hath fed And drunk the milk of Paradise."

[296] Prov. vi. 8, lxx. The reference to the bee is not in the Hebrew.

[297] cf. AElian. v. 13. geometrian de kai kalle schematon kai horaias plaseis auton aneu technes te kai kanonon kai tou kaloumenou hupo ton sophon diabetou, to kalliston schematon hexagonon te kai hexapleuron kai isogonion apodeiknuntai hai melittai.

The Haxaemeron - St Basil

The rows of honey-comb are all hexagonal with equal sides. They do not bear on each other in straight lines, lest the supports should press on empty spaces between and give way; but the angles of the lower hexagons serve as foundations and bases to those which rise above, so as to furnish a sure support to the lower mass, and so that each cell may securely keep the liquid honey. [298]

5. How shall we make an exact review of all the peculiarities of the life of birds? During the night cranes keep watch in turn; some sleep, others make the rounds and procure a quiet slumber for their companions. After having finished his duty, the sentry utters a cry, and goes to sleep, and the one who awakes, in his turn, repays the security which he has enjoyed.[299] You will see the same order reign in their

---

[298] The mathematical exactness of the bee is described by Darwin in terms which make it even more marvellous than it appeared to Basil. "The most wonderful of all known instincts, that of the hive bee, may be explained by natural selection having taken advantage of numerous slight modifications of simpler instincts; natural selection having by slow degrees more and more perfectly led the bees to sweep equal spheres at a given distance from each other in a double layer, and to build up and excavate the wax along the planes of intersection." Origin of Species, ii. 255, ed. 1861. According to this view the beings from whom hive bees, as we know them, are descended were gifted with certain simple instincts capable of a kind of hereditary unconscious education, resulting in a complex instinct which constructs with exact precision the hexagonal chamber best fitted for the purpose it is designed to fulfil, and then packs it. And it is interesting to note how the great apostle of abstract selection personifies it as a "taker" of "advantage," and a "leader."

[299] Arist., Hist. An. ix. 10.

The Haxaemeron - St Basil

flight. One leads the way, and when it has guided the flight of the flock for a certain time, it passes to the rear, leaving to the one who comes after the care of directing the march.

The conduct of storks comes very near intelligent reason. In these regions the same season sees them all migrate. They all start at one given signal. And it seems to me that our crows, serving them as escort, go to bring them back, and to help them against the attacks of hostile birds. The proof is that in this season not a single crow appears, and that they return with wounds, evident marks of the help and of the assistance that they have lent. Who has explained to them the laws of hospitality? Who has threatened them with the penalties of desertion? For not one is missing from the company. Listen, all inhospitable hearts, ye who shut your doors, whose house is never open either in the winter or in the night to travellers. The solicitude of storks for their old would be sufficient, if our children would reflect upon it, to make them love their parents; because there is no one so failing in good sense, as not to deem it a shame to be surpassed in virtue by birds devoid of reason. The storks surround their father, when old age makes his feathers drop off, warm him with their wings, and provide abundantly for his support, and even in their flight they help him as much as they are able, raising him gently on each side upon their wings, a conduct so notorious that it has given to gratitude the name of

The Haxaemeron - St Basil

"antipelargosis."[300] Let no one lament poverty; let not the man whose house is bare despair of his life, when he considers the industry of the swallow. To build her nest, she brings bits of straw in her beak; and, as she cannot raise the mud in her claws, she moistens the end of her wings in water and then rolls in very fine dust and thus procures mud. [301] After having united, little by little, the bits of straw with this mud, as with glue, she feeds her young; and if any one of them has its eyes injured, she has a natural remedy to heal the sight of her little ones.[302]

This sight ought to warn you not to take to evil ways on account of poverty; and, even if you are reduced to the last extremity, not to lose all hope; not to abandon yourself to inaction and idleness, but to have recourse to God. If He is so bountiful to the swallow, what will He not do for those who call upon Him with all their heart?

The halcyon is a sea bird, which lays its eggs along the shore, or deposits them in the sand. And it lays in the middle of winter, when the violence of the winds

---

[300] From pelargos. On the pious affection of the stork, cf. Plato, Alc. i. 135 (S: 61), Arist., H.A. ix. 13, 20, AElian, H.A. iii. 23 and x. 16, and Plin. x. 32. From pelargos was supposed to be derived the Pythagorean word pelargan (Diog. Laert. viii. 20), but this is now regarded as a corruption of pedartan.

[301] "Hirundines luto construunt, stramine roborant: si quando inopia est luti, madefactae multa aqua pennis pulverem spargunt." Plin. x. 49. cf. Arist., Hist. An. ix. 10.

[302] "Chelidoniam visui saluberriman hirundines monstravere, vexatis pullorum oculis illa medentes." Plin. viii. 41. cf. AElian, H.A. iii. 25. Chelidonia is swallowwort or celandine.

The Haxaemeron - St Basil

dashes the sea against the land. Yet all winds are hushed, and the wave of the sea grows calm, during the seven days that the halcyon sits.[303]

For it only takes seven days to hatch the young. Then, as they are in need of food so that they may grow, God, in His munificence, grants another seven days to this tiny animal. All sailors know this, and call these days halcyon days. If divine Providence has established these marvellous laws in favour of creatures devoid of reason, it is to induce you to ask for your salvation from God. Is there a wonder which He will not perform for you—you have been made in His image, when for so little a bird, the great, the fearful sea is held in check and is commanded in the midst of winter to be calm.

6. It is said that the turtle-dove, once separated from her mate, does not contract a new union, but remains in widowhood, in remembrance of her first alliance.[304] Listen, O women! What veneration for widowhood, even in these creatures devoid of reason, how they prefer it to an unbecoming multiplicity of marriages. The eagle shows the greatest injustice in the

---

[303] "Foetificant bruma, qui dies halcyonides vocantur, placido mari per eos et navigabili, Siculo maxime. Plin. x. 47. cf. Arist., H.A. v. 8, 9, and AElian, H. N. i. 36. So Theoc. vii. 57: Ch' halkuones storeseunti ta kumata, tan te thalassan Ton te noton tont' euron hos eschata phukia kinei Sir Thomas Browne (Vulgar Errors) denies the use of a kingfisher as a weather-gauge, but says nothing as to the "halcyon days." Kingfishers are rarely seen in the open sea, but haunt estuaries which are calm without any special miracle. Possibly the halcyon was a tern or sea-swallow, which resembles a kingfisher, but they brood on land.

[304] Arist., H.A. ix. 7.

education which she gives to her young. When she has hatched two little ones, she throws one on the ground, thrusting it out with blows from her wings, and only acknowledges the remaining one. It is the difficulty of finding food which has made her repulse the offspring she has brought forth. But the osprey, it is said, will not allow it to perish, she carries it away and brings it up with her young ones. [305] Such are parents who, under the plea of poverty, expose their children; such are again those who, in the distribution of their inheritance, make unequal divisions. Since they have given existence equally to each of their children, it is just that they should equally and without preference furnish them with the means of livelihood. Beware of imitating the cruelty of birds with hooked talons. When they see their young are from henceforth capable of encountering the air in their flight, they throw them out of the nest, striking them and pushing them with their wings, and do not take the least care of them. The love of the crow for its young is laudable! When they begin to fly, she follows them, gives them food, and for a very long time provides for their nourishment. Many birds have no need of union with males to conceive. But their eggs are unfruitful, except those of vultures, who more

---

[305] Ar. vi. 6 and ix. 34. "Melanaetos…sola aquilarum foetus suos alit; ceterae…fugant." Plin. x. 3. "Pariunt ova terna: excludunt pullos binos: visi sunt et tres aliquando." id. 4, following Musaeus (apud Plutarch, In Mario, p. 426). hos tria men tiktei, duo d' eklepei, hen d' alegizei. On the osprey, see Arist., H.A. ix. 44 and Pliny loc. "Sed ejectos ab his cognatum genus ossifragi excipiunt, et educant cum suis."

The Haxaemeron - St Basil

often, it is said, bring forth without coupling:[306] and this although they have a very long life, which often reaches its hundredth year. Note and retain, I pray you, this point in the history of birds; and if ever you see any one laugh at our mystery, as if it were impossible and contrary to nature that a virgin should become a mother without losing the purity of her virginity, bethink you that He who would save the faithful by the foolishness of preaching, has given us beforehand in nature a thousand reasons for believing in the marvellous.[307]

7. "Let the waters bring forth the moving creatures that have life, and fowl that may fly above the earth in the open firmament of heaven." They received the command to fly above the earth because earth provides them with nourishment. "In the firmament of heaven," that is to say, as we have said before, in that

---

[306] Arist., Hist. An. vi. 6 and ix. 15. So Pliny x. vii. "Nidos nemo attigit: ideo etiam fuere qui putarent illos ex adverso orbe advolare, nidificant enim in excelsissimis rupibus." cf. also AElian, ii. 46: gupa de arrena ou phasi gignesthai pote alla theleias hapasas.

[307] This analogy is repeated almost in identical words in Basil's Hom. xxii. De Providentia. cf. also his Com. on Isaiah. St. Ambrose repeats the illustration (Hex. v. 20). The analogy, even if the facts were true, would be false and misleading. But it is curious to note that were any modern divine desirous of here following in Basil's track, he might find the alleged facts in the latest modern science,—e.g. in the so-called Parthenogenesis, or virginal reproduction, among insects, as said to be demonstrated by Siebold. Haeckel (Hist. of Creation, Lankester's ed. ii. p. 198) represents sexual reproduction as quite a recent development of non-sexual reproduction.

The Haxaemeron - St Basil

part of the air called ouranos, heaven,[308] from the word horan, which means to see;[309] called firmament, because the air which extends over our heads, compared to the aether, has greater density, and is thickened by the vapours which exhale from the earth. You have then heaven adorned, earth beautified, the sea peopled with its own creatures, the air filled with birds which scour it in every direction. Studious listener, think of all these creations which God has drawn out of nothing, think of all those which my speech has left out, to avoid tediousness, and not to exceed my limits; recognise everywhere the wisdom of God; never cease to wonder, and, through every creature, to glorify the Creator.

There are some kinds of birds which live by night in the midst of darkness; others which fly by day in full light. Bats, owls, night-ravens are birds of night: if by chance you cannot sleep, reflect on these nocturnal birds and their peculiarities and glorify their Maker. How is it that the nightingale is always awake when sitting on her eggs, passing the night in a continual melody?[310] How is it that one animal, the bat, is at the same time quadruped and fowl? That it is the only one of the birds to have teeth? That it is viviparous like quadrupeds, and traverses the air, raising itself not

---

[308] cf. note on p. 70.

[309] The Greek word stereoma, from stereos, strong, is traceable to the root star, to spread out, and so indirectly associated with the connotation of the Hebrew rakia.

[310] Arist., H.A. viii. 75. Pliny x. 43. "Luscinus diebus ac noctibus continuis quindecim garrulus sine intermissu cantus, densante se frondium germine, non in novissimum digna miratu ave."

The Haxaemeron - St Basil

upon wings, but upon a kind of membrane?[311] What natural love bats have for each other! How they interlace like a chain and hang the one upon the other! A very rare spectacle among men, who for the greater part prefer individual and private life to the union of common life. Have not those who give themselves up to vain science the eyes of owls? The sight of the owl, piercing during the night time, is dazzled by the splendour of the sun; thus the intelligence of these men, so keen to contemplate vanities, is blind in presence of the true light.

During the day, also, how easy it is for you to admire the Creator everywhere! See how the domestic cock calls you to work with his shrill cry, and how, forerunner of the sun, and early as the traveller, he sends forth labourers to the harvest! What vigilance in geese! With what sagacity they divine secret dangers! Did they not once upon a time save the imperial city? When enemies were advancing by subterranean passages to possess themselves of the capitol of Rome, did not geese announce the danger?[312] Is there any kind of bird whose nature offers nothing for our admiration? Who announces to the vultures that there will be carnage when men march in battle array against one another? You may see flocks of vultures following armies and calculating the result of warlike

---

[311] So also Basil in Hom. on Isaiah iii. 447. cf. Pliny x. 81, "cui et membranaceae pinnae uni."

[312] cf. Livy v. 47 and Plutarch, Camillus, or Verg. viii. 655. The alternative tradition of the mine is preserved by Servius.

The Haxaemeron - St Basil

preparations;[313] a calculation very nearly approaching to human reasoning. How can I describe to you the fearful invasions of locusts, which rise everywhere at a given signal, and pitch their camps all over a country? They do not attack crops until they have received the divine command. Or shall I describe how the remedy for this curse, the thrush, follows them with its insatiable appetite, and the devouring nature that the loving God has given it in His kindness for men?[314] How does the grasshopper modulate its song?[315] Why is it more melodious at midday owing to the air that it breathes in dilating its chest?

But it appears to me that in wishing to describe the marvels of winged creatures, I remain further behind than I should if my feet had tried to match the rapidity of their flight. When you see bees, wasps, in short all those flying creatures called insects, because they have an incision all around, reflect that they have neither respiration nor lungs, and that they are

---

[313] cf. AElian, H.A. ii. 46. kai mentoi kai tais ekdemois stratiais hepontai gupes kai mala ge mantikos hoti eis polemon chorousin eidotes kai hoti mache pasa ergazetai nekrous kai touto egnokotes. cf. Pliny x. 88: "vultures sagacius odorantur."

[314] cf. Galen. vi. 3.

[315] Fialon, quoting the well known ode of Anakreon, "makarizomen se tettix," and Plato's theory of the affection of grasshoppers and the muses in the Phaedrus, contrasts the "cantu querulae rumpent arbusta cicadae" of Vergil (George. iii. 328) and points out that the Romans did not share the Greek admiration for the grasshopper's song.

The Haxaemeron - St Basil

supported by air through all parts of their bodies.[316] Thus they perish, if they are covered with oil, because it stops up their pores. Wash them with vinegar, the pores reopen and the animal returns to life. Our God has created nothing unnecessarily and has omitted nothing that is necessary. If now you cast your eyes upon aquatic creatures, you will find that their organization is quite different. Their feet are not split like those of the crow, nor hooked like those of the carnivora, but large and membraneous; therefore they can easily swim, pushing the water with the membranes of their feet as with oars. Notice how the swan plunges his neck into the depths of the water to draw his food from it, and you will understand the wisdom of the Creator in giving this creature a neck longer than his feet, so that he may throw it like a line, and take the food hidden at the bottom of the water.[317]

8. If we simply read the words of Scripture we find only a few short syllables. "Let the waters bring forth fowl that may fly above the earth in the open firmament of heaven," but if we enquire into the meaning of these words, then the great wonder of the wisdom of the Creator appears. What a difference He

---

[316] "Insecta multi negarunt spirare, idque ratione persuadentes, quoniam in viscera interiora nexus spirabilis non inesset. Itaque vivere ut fruges, arboresque: sed plurimum interesse spiret aliquid an vivat. Eadem de causa nec sanguinem iis esse qui sit nullis carentibus corde atque jecore. Sic nec spirare ea quibus pulmo desit unde numerosa series quaestionum exoritur. Iidem enim et vocem esse his negant, in tanto murmure apium, cicadarum sono...nec video cur magis possint non trahere animam talia, et vivere, quam spirare sine visceribus." Plin. xi. 2.

[317] Arist., De Part. An. iv. 12.

has foreseen among winged creatures! How He has divided them by kinds! How He has characterized each one of them by distinct qualities! But the day will not suffice me to recount the wonders of the air. Earth is calling me to describe wild beasts, reptiles and cattle, ready to show us in her turn sights rivalling those of plants, fish, and birds. "Let the earth bring forth the living soul" of domestic animals, of wild beasts, and of reptiles after their kind. What have you to say, you who do not believe in the change that Paul promises you in the resurrection, when you see so many metamorphoses among creatures of the air? What are we not told of the horned worm of India! First it changes into a caterpillar,[318] then becomes a buzzing insect, and not content with this form, it clothes itself, instead of wings, with loose, broad plates. Thus, O women, when you are seated busy with your weaving, I mean of the silk which is sent you by the Chinese to make your delicate dresses, [319] remember the metamorphoses of this creature, conceive a clear idea of the resurrection, and do not refuse to believe in the change that Paul announces for all men.

But I am ashamed to see that my discourse oversteps the accustomed limits; if I consider the abundance of matters on which I have just discoursed to you, I feel that I am being borne beyond bounds; but when I reflect upon the inexhaustible wisdom which is displayed in the works of creation, I seem to be but at

---

[318] This word is curiously rendered by Eustathius verucae, and by Ambrose caulis. Garnier (Praef. in Bas. 28) thinks that the latter perhaps found in some corrupt ms. kramben for kampen.

[319] Arist., H.A. v. 19.

The Haxaemeron - St Basil

the beginning of my story. Nevertheless, I have not detained you so long without profit. For what would you have done until the evening? You are not pressed by guests, nor expected at banquets. Let me then employ this bodily fast to rejoice your souls. You have often served the flesh for pleasure, to-day persevere in the ministry of the soul. "Delight thyself also in the Lord and he shall give thee the desire of thine heart."[320] Do you love riches? Here are spiritual riches. "The judgments of the Lord are true and righteous altogether. More to be desired are they than gold and precious stones."[321] Do you love enjoyment and pleasures? Behold the oracles of the Lord, which, for a healthy soul, are "sweeter than honey and the honey-comb."[322] If I let you go, and if I dismiss this assembly, some will run to the dice, where they will find bad language, sad quarrels and the pangs of avarice. There stands the devil, inflaming the fury of the players with the dotted bones,[323] transporting the same sums of money from one side of the table to the other, now exalting one with victory and throwing the other into despair, now swelling the first with boasting

---

[320] Ps. xxxvii. 4.

[321] Ps. xix. 9 and 10, LXX.

[322] Ps. xix. 10.

[323] The kuboi were marked on all six sides, the astragaloi on only four, the ends being rounded.

and covering his rival with confusion.[324] Of what use is bodily fasting and filling the soul with innumerable evils? He who does not play spends his leisure elsewhere. What frivolities come from his mouth! What follies strike his ears! Leisure without the fear of the Lord is, for those who do not know the value of time, a school of vice.[325] I hope that my words will be profitable; at least by occupying you here they have prevented you from sinning. Thus the longer I keep you, the longer you are out of the way of evil.

An equitable judge will deem that I have said enough, not if he considers the riches of creation, but if he thinks of our weakness and of the measure one ought to keep in that which tends to pleasure. Earth has welcomed you with its own plants, water with its fish, air with its birds; the continent in its turn is ready to offer you as rich treasures. But let us put an end to this morning banquet, for fear satiety may blunt your taste for the evening one. May He who has filled all with the works of His creation and has left everywhere visible memorials of His wonders, fill your hearts with all spiritual joys in Jesus Christ, our Lord, to whom belong glory and power, world without end. Amen.

---

[324] With Basil's description of the gaming tables, presumably of Caesarea, cf. Ovid's of those of Rome: "Ira subit, deforme malum, lucrique cupido; Jurgiaque et rixae, sollicitusque dolor. Crimina dicuntur, resonat clamoribus aether, Invocat iratos et sibi quisque deos, Nulla fides: tabulaeque novae per vota petuntur, Et lacrymis vidi saepe madere genis. De A.A.iii. 373 seqq.

[325] "Cernis ut ignavum corrumpant otia corpus." Ovid, I. Pont. 6. "Facito aliquid operis ut semper Diabolus inveniat te occupatum. Jerome, In R. Monach.

Homily IX

The creation of terrestrial animals.

1. How did you like the fare of my morning's discourse? It seemed to me that I had the good intentions of a poor giver of a feast, who, ambitious of having the credit of keeping a good table saddens his guests by the poor supply of the more expensive dishes. In vain he lavishly covers his table with his mean fare; his ambition only shows his folly. It is for you to judge if I have shared the same fate. Yet, whatever my discourse may have been, take care lest you disregard it. No one refused to sit at the table of Elisha; and yet he only gave his friends wild vegetables.[326] I know the laws of allegory, though less by myself than from the works of others. There are those truly, who do not admit the common sense of the Scriptures, for whom water is not water, but some other nature, who see in a plant, in a fish, what their fancy wishes, who change the nature of reptiles and of wild beasts to suit their allegories, like the interpreters of dreams who explain visions in sleep to make them serve their own ends. For me grass is grass; plant, fish, wild beast, domestic animal, I take all in the literal sense.[327] "For I am not ashamed of the

---

[326] 2 Kings iv. 39.

[327] Fialon thinks that this plain reference to Origen may have been evoked by some criticisms on the IIIrd Homily. (cf. p. 71) St. Basil's literalism and bold departure from the allegorizing of Origen and from the milder mysticism of Eusebius are remarked on in the Prolegomena.

The Haxaemeron - St Basil

gospel."[328] Those who have written about the nature of the universe have discussed at length the shape of the earth. If it be spherical or cylindrical, if it resemble a disc and is equally rounded in all parts, or if it has the forth of a winnowing basket and is hollow in the middle; [329] all these conjectures have been suggested by cosmographers, each one upsetting that of his predecessor. It will not lead me to give less importance to the creation of the universe, that the servant of God, Moses, is silent as to shapes; he has not said that the earth is a hundred and eighty thousand furlongs in circumference; he has not measured into what extent of air its shadow projects itself whilst the sun revolves around it, nor stated how this shadow, casting itself upon the moon, produces eclipses. He has passed over in silence, as useless, all that is unimportant for us. Shall I then prefer foolish wisdom to the oracles of the Holy Spirit? Shall I not rather exalt Him who, not wishing to fill our minds with these vanities, has regulated all the economy of Scripture in view of the edification and the making perfect of our souls? It is this which those seem to me not to have understood, who, giving themselves up to the distorted meaning of allegory, have undertaken to give a majesty of their own invention to Scripture. It is to believe themselves wiser than the Holy Spirit, and to bring forth their own ideas under a pretext of exegesis. Let us hear Scripture as it has been written.

---

[328] Rom. i. 16.

[329] thales kai hoi Stoikoi kai hoi ap' auton sphairoeide ten gen. 'Anaximandros litho kioni ten gen prosphere ton epipedon. 'Anaximenes, trapezoeide. Leukippos, tumpanoeide. Demokritos, diskoeide men to platei, koilen de to meson. Plut. peri ton aresk. iii. 10. Arist. (De. Coelo ii. 14) follows Thales. So Manilius i. 235: "Ex quo colligitur terrarumforma rotunda."

The Haxaemeron - St Basil

2. "Let the earth bring forth the living creature."[330] Behold the word of God pervading creation, beginning even then the efficacy which is seen displayed to-day, and will be displayed to the end of the world! As a ball, which one pushes, if it meet a declivity, descends, carried by its form and the nature of the ground and does not stop until it has reached a level surface; so nature, once put in motion by the Divine command, traverses creation with an equal step, through birth and death, and keeps up the succession of kinds through resemblance, to the last.[331] Nature always makes a horse succeed to a horse, a lion to a lion, an eagle to an eagle, and preserving each animal by these uninterrupted successions she transmits it to the end of all things. Animals do not see their peculiarities destroyed or effaced by any length of time; their nature, as though it had been just constituted, follows the course of ages, for ever young.[332] "Let the earth bring forth the living creature." This command has continued and earth does not cease to obey the Creator. For, if there are creatures which are successively produced by their predecessors, there are others that even to-day we see born from the earth itself. In wet weather she brings forth grasshoppers and an immense number of insects which fly in the air and have no names because they are so small; she also produces mice and frogs. In the environs of Thebes in Egypt, after abundant rain in hot weather, the country is covered

---

[330] Gen. i. 24.

[331] cf. note on Hom. v. p. 76.

[332] "Sed, si quaeque suo ritu procedit, et omnes Foedere naturae certo discrimina servant." Luc. v. 921.

with field mice.³³³ We see mud alone produce eels; they do not proceed from an egg, nor in any other manner; it is the earth alone which gives them birth.³³⁴ Let the earth produce a living creature."

Cattle are terrestrial and bent towards the earth. Man, a celestial growth, rises superior to them as much by the mould of his bodily conformation as by the dignity of his soul. What is the form of quadrupeds? Their head is bent towards the earth and looks towards their belly, and only pursues their belly's good. Thy head, O man! is turned towards heaven; thy eyes look up.³³⁵ When therefore thou degradest thyself by the passions of the flesh, slave of thy belly, and thy lowest parts, thou approachest animals without reason and becomest like one of them.³³⁶ Thou art called to more noble cares; "seek those things which are above

---

³³³ cf. Plin. ix. 84: Verum omnibus his fidem Nili inundatio affert omnia exedente miraculo: quippe detegente eo musculi reperiuntur inchoato opere genitalis aquae terroeque, jam parte corporis viventes, novissima effigie etiamnum terrena." So Mela De Nilo i. 9. "Glebis etiam infundit animas, ex ipsoque humo vitalia effingit," and Ovid, Met. i. 42: "Sic ubi deseruit madidos septemfluus agros Nilus, et antiquo sua flumina reddidit alveo, AEthereoque recens exarsit sidere limus, Plurima cultores versis animalia glebis Inveniunt."

³³⁴ Arist. H.A. vi. 16. Hai enchelus gignontai ek ton kaloumenon ges enteron ha automata sunistatai en to pelo kai en te ge enikmo. Kai ede eisin ommenai hai men ekdunousai ek touton, hai de en diaknizomenois kai diairoumenois gignontai phanerai.

³³⁵ Arist., Part. An. iv. 10, 18. monon orthon esti ton zoon ho anthropos.

³³⁶ cf. Ps. xlix. 12.

The Haxaemeron - St Basil

where Christ sitteth."[337] Raise thy soul above the earth; draw from its natural conformation the rule of thy conduct; fix thy conversation in heaven. Thy true country is the heavenly Jerusalem;[338] thy fellow-citizens and thy compatriots are "the first-born which are written in heaven."[339]

3. "Let the earth bring forth the living creature." Thus when the soul of brutes appeared it was not concealed in the earth, but it was born by the command of God. Brutes have one and the same soul of which the common characteristic is absence of reason. But each animal is distinguished by peculiar qualities. The ox is steady, the ass is lazy, the horse has strong passions, the wolf cannot be tamed, the fox is deceitful, the stag timid, the ant industrious, the dog grateful and faithful in his friendships. As each animal was created the distinctive character of his nature appeared in him in due measure; in the lion spirit, taste for solitary life, an unsociable character. True tyrant of animals, he, in his natural arrogance, admits but few to share his honours. He disdains his yesterday's food and never returns to the remains of the prey. Nature has provided his organs of voice with such great force that often much swifter animals are caught by his roaring alone. The panther, violent and impetuous in his leaps, has a body fitted for his activity and lightness, in accord with the movements of his soul. The bear has a sluggish nature, ways of its own, a sly character, and is very secret; therefore it

---

[337] Col. iii. 1.

[338] cf. Phil. iii. 20.

[339] Heb. xii. 23.

The Haxaemeron - St Basil

has an analogous body, heavy, thick, without articulations such as are necessary for a cold dweller in dens.

When we consider the natural and innate care that these creatures without reason take of their lives we shall be induced to watch over ourselves and to think of the salvation of our souls; or rather we shall be the more condemned when we are found falling short even of the imitation of brutes. The bear, which often gets severely wounded, cares for himself and cleverly fills the wounds with mullein, a plant whose nature is very astringent. You will also see the fox heal his wounds with droppings from the pine tree; the tortoise, gorged with the flesh of the viper, finds in the virtue of marjoram a specific against this venomous animal[340] and the serpent heals sore eyes by eating fennel.[341]

And is not reasoning intelligence eclipsed by animals in their provision for atmospheric changes? Do we not see sheep, when winter is approaching, devouring grass with avidity as if to make provision for future scarcity? Do we not also see oxen, long confined in the winter season, recognise the return of spring by a natural sensation, and look to the end of their stables towards the doors, all turning their heads there by common consent? Studious observers have remarked that the hedgehog makes an opening at the two

---

[340] Plut. pot. ton. z. k.t.l. chelonai men origanon, galai de peganon, hotan opheos phagosin, epesthiousai. cf. Pliny xx. 68: "Tragoriganum contra viperae ictum efficacissimum."

[341] ho drakon ho to marathro ton ophthalmon ambluoptonta leptunon kai diacharatton. Plut. potera ton z. k.t.l. 731.

The Haxaemeron - St Basil

extremities of his hole. If the wind from the north is going to blow he shuts up the aperture which looks towards the north; if the south wind succeeds it the animal passes to the northern door.[342] What lesson do these animals teach man? They not only show us in our Creator a care which extends to all beings, but a certain presentiment of future even in brutes. Then we ought not to attach ourselves to this present life and ought to give all heed to that which is to come. Will you not be industrious for yourself, O man? And will you not lay up in the present age rest in that which is to come, after having seen the example of the ant? The ant during summer collects treasures for winter. Far from giving itself up to idleness, before this season has made it feel its severity, it hastens to work with an invincible zeal until it has abundantly filled its storehouses. Here again, how far it is from being negligent! With what wise foresight it manages so as to keep its provisions as long as possible! With its pincers it cuts the grains in half, for fear lest they should germinate and not serve for its food. If they are damp it dries them; and it does not spread them out in all weathers, but when it feels that the air will keep of a mild temperature. Be sure that you will never see

---

[342] Ar., Hist. An. ix. 6. peri de tes ton echinon aistheseos sumbebeke pollachou tetheoresthai hoti metaballonton boreon kai noton hoi men en te ge tas opas hauton metameibousi hoi d' en tais oikiais trephomenoi metaballousi pros tous toichous.

rain fall from the clouds so long as the ant has left the grain out.[343]

What language can attain to the marvels of the Creator? What ear could understand them? And what time would be sufficient to relate them? Let us say, then, with the prophet, "O Lord, how manifold are thy works! in wisdom hast thou made them all."[344] We shall not be able to say in self-justification, that we have learnt useful knowledge in books, since the untaught law of nature makes us choose that which is advantageous to us. Do you know what good you ought to do your neighbour? The good that you expect from him yourself. Do you know what is evil? That which you would not wish another to do to you. Neither botanical researches nor the experience of simples have made animals discover those which are useful to them; but each knows naturally what is salutary and marvellously appropriates what suits its nature.

4. Virtues exist in us also by nature, and the soul has affinity with them not by education, but by nature herself. We do not need lessons to hate illness, but by ourselves we repel what afflicts us, the soul has no need of a master to teach us to avoid vice. Now all vice is a sickness of the soul as virtue is its health. Thus those have defined health well who have called

---

[343] huetou poieitai semeion ho Aratos e koiles murmekes oches ex oea panta thasson anenenkanto.' kaitines ouk o& 129; graphousin, alla hina tous apokeimenous karpous hotan eurota sunagontas aisthontai kai phobethosi phthoran kai sepsin anapheronton, huperballei de pasan epinoian suneseos he tou purou tes blasteseos prokatalepsis. Plut. pot. ton. z. k.t.l. 725.

[344] Ps. civ. 24.

it a regularity in the discharge of natural functions; a definition that can be applied without fear to the good condition of the soul. Thus, without having need of lessons, the soul can attain by herself to what is fit

The Haxaemeron - St Basil

and conformable to nature.[345] Hence it comes that

---

[345] This is the Stoic doctrine. "Stoicorum quidem facilis conclusio est; qui cum finem bonorum esse senserint, congruere naturae, cumque ea convenienter vivere." cf. Cic., De Fin. iii. 7, 26, and De Nat. D. i. 14, and Hor., Ep., i. x. 12. "Vivere naturae si convenienter oportet." So the Stoics' main rule of life is homologoumenos te phusei zen. But with Basil this apparent disregard of the doctrine of original sin and the need of grace for redemption must be understood in the light of the catholic doctrine that sin is the corruption of human nature (cf. Art. ix. of Original or Birth Sin), which nature, though corrupt and prone to evil, retains capacities for good. But these capacities do need grace and training. cf. Basil's Homily on Ps. xlv. 166. "What is said about the Saviour had a double sense on account of the nature of the Godhead and the Economy of the incarnation. So, looking to the humanity of God, it is said thou hast loved righteousness and hated iniquity,' instead of saying the rest of men by toil and discipline and careful attention mostly attain a disposition towards good and an aversion from vice. But thou hast a kind of natural relationship to good and alienation from iniquity.' And so to us, if we will, it is not hard to acquire a love of righteousness and a hatred of iniquity." i.e. In Christ, redeemed humanity loves good, and all men naturally' do need toil and discipline. The heredity of sin is recognised by Basil. (e.g. in Hom. in Famen. 7.) Man fell from grace given, and must return to it. (Serm. Ascet. in init.) It must always be remembered that questions of original sin, the will, and grace never had the same importance in the Greek as they had in the Latin church. cf. Dr. Travers Smith on St. Basil (c. ix. p. 108) and Boehringer (Das Vierte Jahrhundert. Basil, p. 102) who remarks: Wenn er auch noch von einer "Wieder herstellung des freien Willens, den wir zu brauchbaren Gefaessen fuer den Herrn und zu jedem guten Werke faehig Werden" (De spir. sanct. 18) spricht, so hat er dies doch nirgends begruendet, obschon er bei der Besprechung der Folgen des Falls zuweilen sich aeussert, es sei der Mensch der von dem Schoepfer erhaltenen Freiheit beraubt worden. Im Allgemeinen setzt er den freien Willen auch nach dem Fall im Menschen so gut wieder Voraus, wie vor dem Fall, so dass jene

The Haxaemeron - St Basil

temperance everywhere is praised, justice is in honour, courage admired, and prudence the object of all aims; virtues which concern the soul more than health concerns the body. Children love[346] your parents, and you, "parents provoke not your children to wrath."[347] Does not nature say the same? Paul teaches us nothing new; he only tightens the links of nature. If the lioness loves her cubs, if the she wolf fights to defend her little ones, what shall man say who is unfaithful to the precept and violates nature herself; or the son who insults the old age of his father; or the father whose second marriage has made him forget his first children?

With animals invincible affection unites parents with children. It is the Creator, God Himself, who substitutes the strength of feeling for reason in them. From whence it comes that a lamb as it bounds from the fold, in the midst of a thousand sheep recognises the colour and the voice of its mother, runs to her, and seeks its own sources of milk. If its mother's udders are dry, it is content, and, without stopping, passes by more abundant ones. And how does the mother recognise it among the many lambs? All have the same voice, the same colour, the same smell, as far at least as regards our sense of smell. Yet there is in these animals a more subtle sense than our perception which makes them recognise their own.[348]

---

[346] In Eph. vi. the word is "obey."

[347] cf. Eph. vi. 4.

[348] Fialon quotes Luc. ii. 367-370: "Praeterea teneri tremulis cum vocibus haedi Cornigeras norunt matres, agnique petulci Balantum pecudes: ita, quod natura reposcit, Ad sua quisque fere decurrunt ubera lactis."

The Haxaemeron - St Basil

The little dog has as yet no teeth, nevertheless he defends himself with his mouth against any one who teases him. The calf has as yet no horns, nevertheless he already knows where his weapons will grow.[349] Here we have evident proof that the instinct of animals is innate, and that in all beings there is nothing disorderly, nothing unforeseen. All bear the marks of the wisdom of the Creator, and show that they have come to life with the means of assuring their preservation.

The dog is not gifted with a share of reason; but with him instinct has the power of reason. The dog has learnt by nature the secret of elaborate inferences, which sages of the world, after long years of study, have hardly been able to disentangle. When the dog is on the track of game, if he sees it divide in different directions, he examines these different paths, and speech alone fails him to announce his reasoning. The creature, he says, is gone here or there or in another direction. It is neither here nor there; it is therefore in the third direction. And thus, neglecting the false tracks, he discovers the true one. What more is done by those who, gravely occupied in demonstrating theories, trace lines upon the dust and

---

[349] cf. Ovid (Halieut. ad init.): "Accepit mundus legem; dedit arma per omnes, Admonuitque sui. Vitulus sic namque minatur, Qui nondum gerit in tenera jam cornua fronte."

The Haxaemeron - St Basil

reject two propositions to show that the third is the true one?[350]

Does not the gratitude of the dog shame all who are ungrateful to their benefactors? Many are said to have fallen dead by their murdered masters in lonely places.[351] Others, when a crime has just been committed, have led those who were searching for the murderers, and have caused the criminals to be brought to justice. What will those say who, not content with not loving the Master who has created them and nourished them, have for their friends men whose mouth attacks the Lord, sitting at the same table with them, and, whilst partaking of their food, blaspheme Him who has given it to them?

5. But let us return to the spectacle of creation. The easiest animals to catch are the most productive. It is on account of this that hares and wild goats produce many little ones, and that wild sheep have twins, for fear lest these species should disappear, consumed by carnivorous animals. Beasts of prey, on the contrary, produce only a few and a lioness with

---

[350] cf. Plutarch (pot. ton z.phr. k.t.l 726). hoi de dialektikoi phasi ton kuna to dia pleionon diezeugmeno chromenon en tois poluschidesin atrapois sullogizesthai pros heauton etoi tende to therion hormeken e tende e tende; alla men oute tende oute tende, tende loipon ara. But the dog is said to smell the first, the second, and the third. If he started off on the third without smelling, he would reason. As it is, there is no "syllogism."

[351] Also taken from Plutarch (potera ton z 726), who tells stories of a dog found by King Pyrrhus on a journey, and of Hesiod's dog.

difficulty gives birth to one lion;[352] because, if they say truly, the cub issues from its mother by tearing her with its claws; and vipers are only born by gnawing through the womb, inflicting a proper punishment on their mother.[353] Thus in nature all has been foreseen, all is the object of continual care. If you examine the members even of animals, you will find that the Creator has given them nothing superfluous, that He has omitted nothing that is necessary. To carnivorous animals He has given pointed teeth which their nature requires for their support. Those that are only half furnished with teeth have received several distinct receptacles for their food. As it is not broken up enough in the first, they are gifted with the power of returning it after it has been swallowed, and it does not assimilate until it has been crushed by rumination. The first, second, third, and fourth stomachs of ruminating animals do not remain idle; each one of them fulfils a necessary function.[354] The neck of the camel is long so that it may lower it to its feet and reach the grass on which it feeds. Bears, lions, tigers, all animals of this sort, have short necks buried in their shoulders; it is because they do not live upon grass and have no need to bend down to the earth;

---

[352] cf. Herod. iii. 108. Aristotle (Hist. An. vi. 31) refutes this.

[353] cf. Pliny (x. 72): "Tertia die intra uterum catulos excludit, deinde singulos singulis diebus parit, viginti fere numero. Itaque ceterae, tarditatis impatientes, perrumpunt latera, occisa parente. cf. Herod. iii. 109. So Prudentius (Hamartigenia 583): "Sic vipera, ut aiunt, Dentibus emoritur fusae per viscera prolis." See Sir T. Browne's Vulgur Errors, iii. 16.

[354] Pliny (xi. 78) says ruminantibus geminus, but this is supposed to be a misreading for quadrigeminus, or a mistaken interpretation of Aristotle (H.A. ii. 19), whom Basil is no doubt following.

The Haxaemeron - St Basil

they are carnivorous and eat the animals upon whom they prey.

Why has the elephant a trunk? This enormous creature, the greatest of terrestrial animals, created for the terror of those who meet it, is naturally huge and fleshy. If its neck was large and in proportion to its feet it would be difficult to direct, and would be of such an excessive weight that it would make it lean towards the earth. As it is, its head is attached to the spine of the back by short vertebrae and it has its trunk to take the place of a neck, and with it it picks up its food and draws up its drink. Its feet, without joints,[355] like united columns, support the weight of its body. If it were supported on lax and flexible legs, its joints would constantly give way, equally incapable of supporting its weight, should it wish either to kneel or rise. But it has under the foot a little ankle joint which takes the place of the leg and knee joints whose mobility would never have resisted this enormous and swaying mass. Thus it had need of this nose which nearly touches its feet. Have you seen them in war marching at the head of the phalanx, like living towers, or breaking the enemies' battalions like mountains of flesh with their irresistible charge? If their lower parts were not in accordance with their size they would never have been able to hold their own. Now we are told that the elephant lives three hundred years and more,[356] another reason for him to have solid and unjointed feet. But, as we have said, his trunk, which has the form and the flexibility of a serpent, takes its food from the earth and raises it up.

---

[355] See Sir T. Browne, Vulgar Errors, iii. 1.

[356] Arist. H.A. viii. 12 and ix. 72. Pliny vii. 10.

Thus we are right in saying that it is impossible to find anything superfluous or wanting in creation. Well! God has subdued this monstrous animal to us to such a point that he understands the lessons and endures the blows we give him; a manifest proof that the Creator has submitted all to our rule, because we have been made in His image. It is not in great animals only that we see unapproachable wisdom; no less wonders are seen in the smallest. The high tops of the mountains which, near to the clouds and continually beaten by the winds, keep up a perpetual winter, do not arouse more admiration in me than the hollow valleys, which escape the storms of lofty peaks and preserve a constant mild temperature. In the same way in the constitution of animals I am not more astonished at the size of the elephant, than at the mouse, who is feared by the elephant, or at the scorpion's delicate sting, which has been hollowed like a pipe by the supreme artificer to throw venom into the wounds it makes. And let nobody accuse the Creator of having produced venomous animals, destroyers and enemies of our life. Else let them consider it a crime in the schoolmaster when he disciplines the restlessness of youth by the use of the rod and whip to maintain order.[357]

6. Beasts bear witness to the faith. Hast thou confidence in the Lord? "Thou shalt walk upon the asp and the basilisk and thou shalt trample under feet the lion and the dragon."[358] With faith thou hast the power to walk upon serpents and scorpions. Do you not see that the viper which attached itself to the hand

---

[357] cf. Hom. v. 4.

[358] cf. Ps. xci. 13.

of Paul, whilst he gathered sticks, did not injure him, because it found the saint full of faith? If you have not faith, do not fear beasts so much as your faithlessness, which renders you susceptible of all corruption. But I see that for a long time you have been asking me for an account of the creation of man, and I think I can hear you all cry in your hearts, We are being taught the nature of our belongings, but we are ignorant of ourselves. Let me then speak of it, since it is necessary, and let me put an end to my hesitation. In truth the most difficult of sciences is to know one's self. Not only our eye, from which nothing outside us escapes, cannot see itself; but our mind, so piercing to discover the sins of others, is slow to recognise its own faults.[359] Thus my speech, after eagerly investigating what is external to myself, is slow and hesitating in exploring my own nature. Yet the beholding of heaven and earth does not make us know God better than the attentive study of our being does; I am, says the Prophet, fearfully and wonderfully made;[360] that is to say, in observing myself I have known Thy infinite wisdom.[361] And God said "Let us make man."[362] Does not the light of theology shine, in these words, as through windows;

---

[359] cf. St. Matt. vii. 3.

[360] cf. Ps. cxxxix. 14.

[361] "E coelo descendit gnothi seauton" (Juv. xi. 27). Socrates, Chilo, Thales, Cleobulus, Bias, Pythagoras, have all been credited with the saying. "On reconnait ici le precepte fecond de l'ecole socratique. L'eglise chretienne s'en empara comme de tout ce qu'elle trouvait de grand et de bon dans l'ancienne Grece. Fialon. St. Basil has a Homily on the text proseche seauto (Deut. xv. 9, lxx.)

[362] Gen. i. 26.

The Haxaemeron - St Basil

and does not the second Person show Himself in a mystical way, without yet manifesting Himself until the great day? Where is the Jew who resisted the truth and pretended that God was speaking to Himself? It is He who spoke, it is said, and it is He who made. "Let there be light and there was light." But then their words contain a manifest absurdity. Where is the smith, the carpenter, the shoemaker, who, without help and alone before the instruments of his trade, would say to himself; let us make the sword, let us put together the plough, let us make the boot? Does he not perform the work of his craft in silence? Strange folly, to say that any one has seated himself to command himself, to watch over himself, to constrain himself, to hurry himself, with the tones of a master! But the unhappy creatures are not afraid to calumniate the Lord Himself. What will they not say with a tongue so well practised in lying? Here, however, words stop their mouth; "And God said let us make man." Tell me; is there then only one Person? It is not written "Let man be made," but, "Let us make man." The preaching of theology remains enveloped in shadow before the appearance of him who was to be instructed, but, now, the creation of man is expected, that faith unveils herself and the dogma of truth appears in all its light. "Let us make man." O enemy of Christ, hear God speaking to His Co-operator, to Him by Whom also He made the worlds, Who upholds all things by the word of His power.[363] But He does not leave the voice of true religion without answer. Thus the Jews, race hostile to truth, when they find themselves pressed, act like beasts enraged against man, who roar at the bars of their cage and show the cruelty and the ferocity of

---

[363] cf. Heb. i. 2, 3.

The Haxaemeron - St Basil

their nature, without being able to assuage their fury. God, they say, addresses Himself to several persons; it is to the angels before Him that He says, "Let us make man." Jewish fiction! a fable whose frivolity shows whence it has come. To reject one person, they admit many. To reject the Son, they raise servants to the dignity of counsellors; they make of our fellow slaves the agents in our creation. The perfect man attains the dignity of an angel; but what creature can be like the Creator? Listen to the continuation. "In our image." What have you to reply? Is there one image of God and the angels? Father and Son have by absolute necessity the same form, but the form is here understood as becomes the divine, not in bodily shape, but in the proper qualities of Godhead. Hear also, you who belong to the new concision[364] and who, under the appearance of Christianity, strengthen the error of the Jews.[365] To Whom does He say, "in our image," to whom if it is not to Him who is "the brightness of His glory and the express image of His person,"[366] "the image of the invisible God"?[367] It is then to His living image, to Him Who has said "I and my Father are one,"[368] "He that hath seen me hath seen the Father,"[369] that God says "Let us make man

---

[364] Phil. iii. 2.

[365] The Arians.

[366] Heb. i. 3.

[367] Col. i. 15.

[368] John x. 30.

[369] John xiv. 9.

in our image." Where is the unlikeness[370] in these Beings who have only one image? "So God created man."[371] It is not "They made." Here Scripture avoids the plurality of the Persons. After having enlightened the Jew, it dissipates the error of the Gentiles in putting itself under the shelter of unity, to make you understand that the Son is with the Father, and guarding you from the danger of polytheism. He created him in the image of God. God still shows us His co-operator, because He does not say, in His image, but in the image of God.

If God permits, we will say later in what way man was created in the image of God, and how he shares this resemblance. Today we say but only one word. If there is one image, from whence comes the intolerable blasphemy of pretending that the Son is unlike the Father? What ingratitude! You have yourself received this likeness and you refuse it to your Benefactor! You pretend to keep personally that which is in you a gift of grace, and you do not wish that the Son should keep His natural likeness to Him who begat Him.

But evening, which long ago sent the sun to the west, imposes silence upon me. Here, then, let me be content with what I have said, and put my discourse to bed. I have told you enough up to this point to excite your zeal; with the help of the Holy Spirit I will make for you a deeper investigation into the truths which follow. Retire, then, I beg you, with joy, O

---

[370] to anomoion. Arius had taught that the Persons are anomoioi pampan allelon.

[371] Gen. i. 27.

The Haxaemeron - St Basil

Christ-loving congregation, and, instead of sumptuous dishes of various delicacies, adorn and sanctify your tables with the remembrance of my words. May the Anomoean be confounded, the Jew covered with shame, the faithful exultant in the dogmas of truth, and the Lord glorified, the Lord to Whom be glory and power, world without end. Amen.

Made in the USA
Monee, IL
23 August 2019